Prai... [barcode: D0189252]

I have thoroughly enjoyed readin... ...nd
personal, and peppered with insp... ...ies.
The practical ideas are super. It is ... inspirational book to help us think
about how we can develop a healthy, flexible, engaging and kind response to
relationships in our every changing world, within the core settings of the
work place, our homes, communities and our schools. It will be such a useful
resource for anyone!

Caro Strover, Chartered Educational Psychologist

Reading *Grow* is like chatting with a friend. Deceptively straightforward and
upbeat, Jackie's narrative demystifies the scientific, philosophical and
psychological theories that she believes underpin human happiness, linking
ideas, telling stories and ultimately offering readers their own powerful path
to positivity: thinking on purpose. Really accessible, fun and thought-
provoking, this book is definitely a life changer.

Lisa Stone, Head of Coaching, Professional Tutor
and Teacher of English, Akeley Wood School

Jackie Beere sets out to write a really practical book, full of gentle advice and
free from jargon or technical terms: this is exactly what she has done. The
most useful research and writing from over the last two decades – from the
worlds of education, neuroscience, positive and cognitive psychology –
have been woven together in an easy-to-read, down-to-earth book that will
appeal to anybody interested in personal change.

Jackie makes an important case for 'growth' becoming the natural exten-
sion of 'learning to learn'; that if we understand how our brains work, we can
become much more purposeful with our understanding and unlock our
true potential. Mindset, emotional intelligence and behavioural science are
used to cr... ...compelling
is the wa... ...ift in some
respects, ... Imagine an

education system where personal growth is the main driver – all of a sudden, knowledge acquisition is no longer enough and young people's mental health matters as much as anything else. Hurray! However, this book is certainly not for educators alone. Aspiring to be happier, healthier and more productive in our relationships is something most of us strive for. This book shines a light on our current behaviours and offers us the choice of a possible new reality that we have the power to shape. Without judgement, and often using personal stories, Jackie offers alternative ways of dealing with very familiar situations, ways which ensure that we learn and grow stronger and more resilient. She also offers us the opportunity not only to affect change in ourselves but to support change in others by using coaching techniques.

Jackie does not pretend to offer anything radically new, but what she does do, with great humility, is offer a much needed, straightforward reminder of some incredibly powerful approaches that all parents, teachers, employees and employers cannot do without. I wish I could give this book to everyone I know!

Manjit Shellis, Director of Learning, University of the First Age

Inspiring and upbeat – felt the positive practical coaching throughout. Full of useful exercises and practical tips that help develop insight into behaviour. The most awesome element is discovering that real change is actually achievable – even I am convinced. I can do this!

Maureen Floyd, Children's Social Work Manager

Reading *Grow* was a turning point for me when I was going through a crisis of meaning in my life. In terms of conventional success – a well-paid professional job, a very happy family, a good social network, fulfilling hobbies – I seemed to have it all. But somehow I felt deeply, profoundly unfulfilled. I struggled with this feeling for many years as I travelled in trains, planes and cars from client to client. I felt ungrateful for the bountiful existence fate had chanced to serve me and that I didn't seem to want. I tried to knuckle down and 'make lemonade from the lemons'. Then it all got too much, and I got to thinking seriously about my life. I realised I was judging 'success' the wrong way. I was using someone else's definition of success, not my own. I sat down and wrote out what success really meant to me, and what it did not mean. I created my own success manifesto which helped me see that I was judging myself on totally the wrong benchmarks.

Over time I started to reset my life to fit in with my ideas of success, not anyone else's. It was not – and still is not – an easy journey, because we are all hard-wired by society, consumerism and education to define success as certain attributes. We think of success in very specific, limited terms such as our profession, looks, wealth and possessions. We don't stop to think of success in terms of wisdom gained, friendships made or moments experienced. Gradually I have started to loosen the tethers that bind me to one idea of success and align my whole life with another better idea, one that fits with how I feel deep inside. There is no way that I can tell anyone what success really means to them personally, but I do hope you can use *Grow* to help you find your own specific definition of success and, with the help of Jackie's guidance throughout the book, move towards it with confidence and bravery.

Robert Beere, a more contented individual

We all seek happiness, but the question many people never ask themselves is ... what does happiness look like for me? I found the happiness manifesto in Jackie Beere's *Grow* very insightful in helping me to identify what happiness looks like to me. I was able to see the areas in my life which were incongruent and then look to make the changes I needed. It sounds so simple but it has been by far the most effective tool in my personal growth journey.

Sangeeta Sami, Digital Marketing Consultant

This is a great book which offers a practical and realistic approach to self-development. It proves an inspiring, insightful and intelligent approach to personal learning, which explains what holds us back and how to get on with the journey. Well worth a read.

Steph Coleman, IT and Customer Experience Director, Microlease

A well-judged balance between the academic, the informative and the anecdotal makes this an engaging, absorbing and accessible read. A book that brings together a plethora of current thinking and delivers a strong central message about our ability to grow as people – full of practical advice, tools for self-testing, excellent summaries and a clever device to answer the sceptics' questions. A book to make you think, but so full of optimism and positivity it's hard not to smile as well!

Rhona MacDonald, Accountant and Management Consultant

Grow is a treasure-trove of ideas and insights into why we think, react and interpret the world in the ways we do. This fantastic book unpacks findings from the fields of cognitive psychology, personal development and self-help and gives us immediate and practical ways to use them in our own lives. With *Grow*, everything is gathered in one place, drawing together great ideas and valuable lessons from leading thinkers, scientists and business gurus, all focused on helping the reader set their own path and fulfil their goals.

With helpful self-reflection questionnaires, real-life stories and practical advice, *Grow* is a book for everyone with an interest in learning more about themselves, their colleagues, family, partners and society. *Grow* will help any interested reader to take their next steps, set their next goals and face their next challenges.

Zoë Elder, Executive Director, Clevedon Learning Hub,
Independent Education Consultant and author of *Full On Learning*

GROW

Change your mindset, change your life

A practical guide to thinking on purpose

JACKIE BEERE

Crown House Publishing Limited

www.crownhouse.co.uk

First published by

Crown House Publishing Ltd
Crown Buildings, Bancyfelin, Carmarthen, Wales, SA33 5ND, UK
www.crownhouse.co.uk

and

Crown House Publishing Company LLC
PO Box 2223, Williston, VT 05495
www.crownhousepublishing.com

British Library Cataloguing-in-Publication Data
A catalogue entry for this book is available
from the British Library.

Print ISBN 978-1-78583-011-2
Mobi ISBN 978-1-78583-048-8
ePub ISBN 978-1-78583-049-5
ePDF ISBN 978-1-78583-050-1

LCCN 2015953359

Printed and bound in the UK by
TJ International, Padstow, Cornwall

This book is dedicated to my dad,
who loved to learn new things.

Contents

Introduction

'In the 21st century, it is not the *strongest* people that thrive, nor the most intelligent, but those *who respond best to change and choose to grow.*'

As a teacher, writer, trainer, mother, wife, friend, worrier and optimist, I have been on a lifelong journey of self-discovery to see how to make life work well so that I can be both happy *and* successful. On the way I've experienced massive challenges and tragic events alongside unexpected achievements. My lifelong action research project has been to find out how to survive – and thrive.

I've discovered over and over again that the key to successful living and happy relationships depends on the way you think when you react to events.

We will all experience our share of tragedy and triumph – think, for example, of Amy Winehouse and Katie Piper. Different people, different outcomes. The difference between them is in how they reacted to events. Do you turn triumph into tragedy – or tragedy into triumph?

In order to move on in life, we have to adapt constantly to what happens around us – and *to* us. Our ability to cope well in a changing world is an essential element of a happy existence. How we react to events or respond to changes, both minor and major, determines whether or not we will experience success or failure in life.

Our response to change and to events affects what happens next.

And that becomes the beginning of the next stage of our journey.

From thinking to feeling, then acting

The way you think impacts on the way you communicate, both internally and with others. The way you think creates habits and attitudes that influence your behaviour. The way you think helps you choose to grow – or not.

Thoughts can make you feel happy or sad, clever or stupid, beautiful or ugly – despite all the physical or other evidence to the contrary. What I call 'thinking on purpose' is a method of helping you understand and manage your feelings; a method that grows the emotional intelligence (EQ) you need to become happier, wiser, kinder and more successful.

This book aims to share some observations, stories and practical tools to help you, and others you care about, grow to become more resilient and adaptable. Thinking on purpose means managing your thoughts, and therefore your feelings, effectively. It's a personal perspective, but one that is informed by wide reading and research. I have been particularly inspired by Daniel Goleman's work on emotional intelligence, Carol Dweck's research on the power of developing a growth mindset, the founding principles of neuro-linguistic programming, and the latest discoveries about our brains and how they work.

The journey into learning

It all begins with thinking.

What is thinking? We all think – it's hard not to! Surely we don't need a book to tell us how to do something we do all day long? According to Daniel Kahneman, we speak about 16,000 words a day, but we think using up to five times that many words.[1] Our minds run a constant dialogue or commentary on the sights and sounds, highs and lows that we experience. And most of the time we're not even aware of it. But this inner dialogue is often forming our reactions, creating our attitudes and shaping our behaviours … and we don't realise it is having this effect.

Your thoughts might flit from food to television, to animals, to work, to friends, to the weather – all in the twinkling of an eye. If you tried to stop thinking, the word 'stop' would start a whole new set of connections. One thing is for sure: if I say, 'Don't think of an elephant', an elephant will be the only thing you can think of!

This means 'thinking on purpose' can be tough because we have to learn to manage the pictures and words that create meaning for us. Creating meaning elicits a response; a response that feeds our emotions and beliefs. Thoughts really do change minds!

Understanding how we think, and acknowledging the chaos that reigns in our heads, helps us to challenge the way we sometimes think, and find out how to think on purpose in more systematic, productive ways. We can reframe how we see situations by thinking on purpose and develop a cognitive flexibility that will build our resilience and confidence.

How do you see learning?

For many people, the idea of 'learning' has negative associations. It started off well as you sauntered through your babyhood and early learning journeys into walking, talking, climbing and exploring. Sooner or later, though, someone judges you, measures your progress, and compares you to others. School does this constantly, with tests

---

1   D. Kahneman, *Thinking, Fast and Slow* (London: Penguin, 2011).

and exams – or even on the sports field you can be left feeling stupid or embarrassed when you struggle in front of your peers. It is easy to stop enjoying learning.

As an ex-teacher, I know that the school system isn't perfect in terms of teaching or developing the habits of great learning in our children. Schools are often too bound up in systems, delivering Ofsted's demands, measuring progress, quality control, exam results and all the rest. They often forget that the best learning comes from taking a risk and making mistakes. This can leave a legacy – and for many not a very positive one. This experience can make learning later in life more of a struggle. As they have not developed an understanding of learning, people then have to overcome the emotional barriers to learning that may have been generated at school.

Still, once you leave school you have the chance to take charge of your own learning. You can choose to learn at work or at home by reading, taking up hobbies, learning to play sport or music, or simply by watching others who are good at things. You can keep on growing new neural pathways until the day you die. Or you can *choose* to do none of these.

I'm not a psychologist or a neuroscientist, but I am fascinated by people and how they can change. I've been on many different kinds of training course, and read all the latest self-help books. My bookshelves at home tell the story of each of my decades. What did I try? Well, I explored a number of personal development theories which I'll mention throughout this book, because some have worked for me. Some may also work for you, but taming your brain will be hard work and there is no quick fix. It is more like a lifelong journey.

Where this book came from

As I've said, lots of reading has informed this book, but my main inspirations have been:

- Daniel Goleman's work on emotional intelligence
- Richard Bandler and John Grinder's concept of neuro-linguistic programming (NLP), and
- Carol Dweck's work on mindsets.

Emotional intelligence

Daniel Goleman's work encouraged me to consider the following as the driving forces of success:

- *Managing emotions.* For me, this involves being able to control my instinctive emotional reaction to a situation so that I avoid acting on impulse; being able to stand back for a few moments and take stock of a situation before I think, say or do something that is inspired by fear or anger. Losing your temper – with yourself or others – can become an unhelpful habit. Managing your emotions so they don't control you requires thinking on purpose!
- *Self-awareness.* This is a basic requirement if you are going to be able to manage your emotions. You must understand your emotions, what they feel like, where they come from and how they help – or hinder – you.
- *Self-motivation.* What makes you want to do anything? I am motivated by ticking off a list of jobs, and feeling I've finished them; by making a difference to other people, and seeing them grow; by doing something I'm scared of and surprising myself. It's also enjoying simple things like riding to the shops on my bike to get the groceries. What motivates you?
- *Deferred gratification.* Being able to do the 'worst' thing on your list

of jobs first means you are able to defer your gratification. All learning requires deferred gratification because you have to go through the pain to get the gain. Goleman writes about the 'marshmallow test',[2] in which young children are told that they can have one marshmallow now or, if they wait fifteen minutes, they can have two marshmallows. Some children as young as five were found to have the ability to distract themselves from eating the first marshmallow, to get the reward. These children are already practising thinking on purpose because they can consider how to put off what they want now to get something better later. This skill makes these children more likely to succeed at school, stick with relationships, and resist drugs and drink. I will return to this in more detail throughout the book.

■ *Managing relationships.* The key to happiness for so many people is friends and family – yet friends and family can also be a source of great unhappiness. For me, managing relationships is about understanding – *really* understanding – other people's point of view. This is explored in Chapters 7 and 8. It is so important to realise that making other people happy will make you happy. The journey from selfishness to kindness and selflessness is a common theme in many films and dramas, from Shakespeare's Shylock in *The Merchant of Venice* to Scrooge in Dickens' *A Christmas Carol*.

Neuro-linguistic programming

Richard Bandler and John Grinder, who first developed neuro-linguistic programming (NLP), wanted to produce a practical manual to show how anyone could become excellent at something by studying the habits of others who excelled in their field.[3] They found

---

2   D. Goleman, *Emotional Intelligence: Why it can matter more than IQ* (London: Bloomsbury, 1996).

3   J. Grinder and R. Bandler, *Frogs into Princes: Neuro linguistic programming* (Moab, UT: Real People Press, 1981).

lots of people who did things really well and analysed exactly what they did, so that this could be replicated by anyone. In the process, they encountered or created a number of general rules that seemed to be common to these people, and which Bandler and Grinder found useful in understanding other people, the world and how to succeed. For example:

- There is no such thing as failure, only feedback – this is a mantra which I'll often refer to later, along with the others below.
- The map is not the territory – this is useful to remind you that, even though you see a situation a certain way, other people may have a different view.
- The meaning of your communication is the response you get – a warning to pay attention to the effect you are having on others.
- Everyone has the resources inside them to achieve anything they want – a reminder that, when you meet a challenge, the first place to look for solutions is within yourself.
- Every behaviour has a positive intention – people do things for their own reasons. The fact that their value system is different from yours doesn't mean they are wrong and you are right. What you need to do is unravel the thought processes that led them to the decision to act in a certain way.

These interesting presuppositions are worth considering, and have underpinned much of my own thinking. They will be explored in more detail throughout this book.

Growth mindsets

More recently, the psychologist Carol Dweck has risen to the fore through her work with children and their mindsets.[4] She believes that, in order to achieve the very best outcomes in learning, you need to concentrate on the way you think about yourself and respond to others: this has a massive impact on how well you will fulfil your potential.

She distinguishes between the growth mindset and the fixed mindset. Having a growth mindset means you:

- believe intelligence can grow
- prioritise learning over everything else, including results
- see mistakes or failure as a challenge and an opportunity to improve
- are inspired by other people's success and the chance to learn from them
- always want to push yourself outside your comfort zone in order to grow.

In contrast, having a fixed mindset means you:

- believe intelligence is fixed – you have a certain IQ and that's that
- need to prove yourself over and over
- tend to avoid challenges when the outcome is uncertain and you may be seen to fail
- feel threatened by negative feedback, even when it is meant constructively
- think you're smart, so you shouldn't have to try as hard – effort is for the less intelligent.

---

4   C. Dweck, *Mindset: The new psychology of success* (New York: Random House, 2007).

I'll cover the implications of these different mindsets in Chapter 5.

My aim was to write a book that was free from jargon and technical terms but full of practical advice and personal stories that may help nudge your thinking to create more cognitive flexibility. If you can think in different ways, you can adapt your responses and create the outcome you want.

The relentless application of 'thinking on purpose' in my work and in my career as a teacher, and at home as a parent and wife, has probably driven my students and family crazy at times – but you know what? It works!

I wish you the best of luck exploring how this book could help you think and grow.

Jackie Beere OBE

Chapter 1

Why we need to grow

'Once you stop learning, you may as well stop living.'

Derrick Beere[1]

'We must continually remind ourselves that there is a difference between what is natural and what is actually good for us.'

Sam Harris[2]

GROW: Produce, mature, expand, sprout, cultivate, flourish, thrive, develop, raise, nurture

---

I have discovered that the most important strategy for being happy and successful in work and in life is to consciously decide to be open-minded and flexible enough to grow through learning. In this book I use the term 'grow' to mean developing a mindset[3] (attitude, outlook, way of thinking) that will help you navigate through the trials and tribulations of life, and still maintain your desire and ability to keep learning.

---

1   This was one of my father's favourite sayings.
2   S. Harris, *The Moral Landscape* (London: Bantam Press, 2010), p. 101.
3   See Dweck, *Mindset*.

Choosing to grow is learning, in the widest sense of the word. It means developing new skills and knowledge, but also finding out about yourself and how you can communicate more effectively and manage your emotions. By doing this, I suggest, you are far more likely to feel happy and contented, achieve your potential and do things you never thought possible.

Choosing to grow ensures that everything we learn makes us stronger, wiser, more emotionally intelligent, and happier, healthier members of society. What's not to like?

If we are good at learning, we can be more capable and comfortable with change – which, in our uncertain world, seems like a no-brainer. However, it is a lifelong challenge to keep learning from your good and bad experiences and then adapt your behaviour when you need to. Too often, we end up repeating the same mistakes, or find ourselves in a spiral of unhelpful habits that holds us back. For example, you may have a habit of arriving late wherever you go. You want to get there on time, but somehow there is always a last-minute distraction, phone call, email to check, or mascara that gets smudged. You promise yourself you will change and allow yourself more time, but at the same time there is another part of you that thinks, 'Oh well, that's just me – I'm a "late" person – everyone knows that and understands.' So you get later and later until, one day, you miss a plane, interview or date – one that really matters.

To change unhelpful habits and beliefs takes hard work – but doing the work becomes increasingly satisfying. To *choose* to work out why you are stuck and how to better move forward with the big, important stuff as well as the minutiae of life – that is part of the process of growing. It is not a once-and-for-all thing, but a lifelong challenge in which you constantly learn from your mistakes and change behaviours that are not working.

Learning applies across the board: at work, in relationships, in families – wherever we encounter frustrations and difficulties which, unattended, can gnaw away at and undermine our contentment. When all our instincts, beliefs and emotions are urging us to do what we have always done, to stick to what feels safe and familiar, then we can find ourselves trapped by those bad habits or limiting beliefs. We know from looking around us that, despite our material wealth, many of us aren't very happy or mentally healthy – and this starts when we are young.

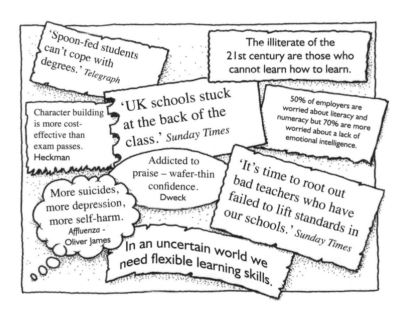

Figure 1.1: What are our schools teaching?

I've shown the snippets of newspaper headlines in Figure 1.1 many times when I've been training teachers and leaders, to encourage discussion about the need to develop a culture for growth in our schools and organisations. It seems obvious to me that our success is linked to our ability to continue learning and growing our social and emotional skills, so why isn't it absolutely endemic in our society or taught in our schools? What is stopping us from fulfilling our potential? Why are so many people unhappy, mentally ill, see threats everywhere, or are just plain scared of what might happen next?

Our world seems to be full of stories of children who self-harm by cutting, using drugs or starving themselves. There are adults who drink, eat and smoke too much. There are people and groups who hate others, who maintain old enmities over decades – even centuries. It is no wonder that our view of the world can be somewhat depressing.

Yet I remain an unrelenting optimist. Despite all the evidence that suggests human beings are wretched, I believe that things will turn out well. I know that awful things are happening, but I am also familiar with the other side: the children who work tirelessly to raise money for good causes, the people who survive appalling abuse or injury and are determined to lead productive lives, and the groups who cooperate and collaborate to build their communities. Seeing the good in other people and the world is part of my habitual, unconscious outlook, so it's not too difficult for me to wake up in the morning, pull the curtains back with a cheery smile, and feel happy about the day ahead. Most of the time this is a virtuous circle, and I get my positive outlook reflected back to me.

One of the most important challenges I ever had was given to me at a training event when I was in my early twenties. I was told to 'Try and make sure that everyone you come into contact with walks away from you feeling a little bit happier.' So have I learned to be an optimist through years of self-coaching? Did I have to put in the effort and the practice, or was I born with this predisposition? Is it my own default setting, programmed through my genes?

I would say that my mindset is due to a mixture of these things. Although there could be a genetic influence, this still doesn't mean that anyone's mindset is fixed for life. Recent research into epigenetics[4] has shown that there are aspects of our genetic make-up that are only triggered given the right conditions. In other words, the possibility of change and adaptation is built in, whoever you started life as. As Oliver James says in his recent book *Not in Your Genes,* there is a case for nurture overcoming nature in determining how your personality develops throughout your life.[5]

If I didn't believe you can change, whatever you think your default setting might be, then I wouldn't be writing this book.

For many people, even in affluent, peaceful Western societies, times have been tough over the last few years. But, relatively speaking, life, for almost everyone, is better than it ever has been. Compared to life one hundred years ago, or to the suffering in war-torn countries, people in these societies have never had it so good. Can you remember the days before mobile phones, Facebook and the internet? Was life better or worse without social media, online shopping, and video on demand? It was certainly different. Given all these aids to better communication and connectedness, we need to ask *why* more and more people feel isolated, depressed, anxious and unhappy. Suicide is the biggest killer of men under fifty. Our prisons are full of people with mental health issues – in a Ministry of Justice study, 49% of female and 23% of male prisoners were assessed as suffering from anxiety and depression[6] – and stress is often cited as a cause of employment difficulties. In *Affluenza* (2007), Oliver James says that many societies with less material wealth than ours have happier citizens, so a lack of money does not guarantee unhappiness.[7] In fact, some of the wealthiest people seem distinctly unable to use their money to make themselves happy. Imagine you won the lottery. What would you care about?

---

4   N. Carey, *The Epigenetics Revolution* (London: Icon Books, 2011).
5   O. James, *Not in Your Genes* (London: Vermilion, 2016).
6   See www.prisonreformtrust.org.uk/projectsresearch/mentalhealth.
7   O. James, *Affluenza* (London: Vermilion, 2007).

Preserving your fortune? Would you fret about what to spend it on? Or would you increase it by making investments? All of these issues are great opportunities for worrying, and can be seen as burdens.

So what is the secret of happiness?

As a child I was outgoing, gregarious, a little bit naughty and 'alternative', and also an introspective extrovert. I did crazy, loud things then spent hours thinking over what I had said or done – often regretting it. That tension between our public and private selves I will explore later, but I think this conflict is what led to my first trauma, a fear of public speaking which hit me like a hammer in my late teens. At first my main coping strategies were avoidance, denial and escape – 'I don't want to do it and I won't do it'. Privately, I read up about anxiety, mind management and positive thinking. Eventually I attended courses on NLP, paid for hypnotherapy, and joined a public speaking support group. Unknowingly, I had set out on a lifelong quest to grow the mindset that would make me happy, and able to learn from my mistakes, and find out what works for me.

The secret, I found, was to *choose to grow*. By this I mean I chose to keep challenging myself to do things that were outside my comfort zone. To do something that scared me every day. To learn new skills and knowledge, find new ways to do things, explore ideas, invent solutions, create art and music, rise to challenges, either on my own or alongside others. It's hard to be gloomy when you're in a learning state of mind. Why? Because your focus is not on yourself or your emotional state, but on what you are doing. Your attention is outwards, not inwards.

So is it easy to 'just get learning' and grow? No, because it exposes our weaknesses and makes us feel vulnerable, or even stupid.

All too often our experiences at school made learning feel more like pain than pleasure. Consequently, some of us developed limiting beliefs at an early age about our potential to rise to learning challenges. Even now, many of us don't consider ourselves to be great learners

– think back to the time you decided to try to learn to speak a new language or learn to play a musical instrument. We often feel reluctant to leave our comfort zone and become the lifelong learners we need to be. We would rather think we can't do something, rather than choose to think 'I can't do that – yet!'

Connect to your inner baby

Who are naturally the happiest people on the planet, as long as their basic needs are met? Young children. Picture a one-year-old discovering how to stack bricks and then watching them fall over time after time. Or toddlers taking their first tentative steps, delighted to be upright and on the brink of freedom. One of the things that makes young children so happy is the intrinsic joy of overcoming learning challenges. They haven't yet learned to become sensitive to the judgement of others, or aware of what success and failure mean. Adults see this early learning and think of the child creating new neural pathways; connecting knowledge to gain an understanding of how things work. For the child, it is pure enjoyment.

Children in their early years are generally wired to be avid, relentless learners, driven by curiosity to learn through play. Provided they are healthy and experience emotional connection with another they have no hang-ups about falling over, making mistakes, getting it wrong, looking foolish or being judged inadequate. They may feel frustrated, feel pain and have preferences, but their basic desires in life are to be loved, make emotional connections with others, and to learn. Curiosity about how things work makes them explore or stare. Determination makes them practise things over and over again and take huge risks – often without considering risk assessment procedures! Just watch a two-year-old fearlessly launch herself at a flight of stairs. Three-year-olds ask endless questions, but by the time children are older, often around eleven or twelve, they may have lost their curiosity or become too self-conscious to ask.

Being good at change and adapting to new challenges is all about learning new approaches and strategies. This is what healthy, happy babies instinctively and endlessly do all the time. We – and our growing children – need to keep in touch with our 'inner baby' aptitude for learning if we are to thrive (Figure 1.2).

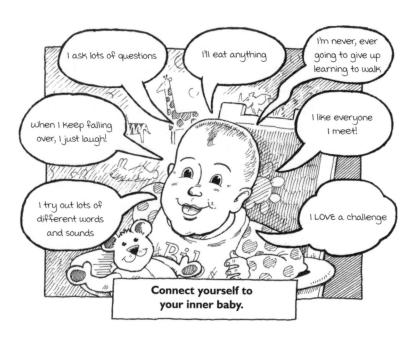

Figure 1.2: Connect to your inner baby.

What happens to this natural inclination to love learning? If we all have that basic instinct to learn and grow, then why do some of us lose our instinctive enjoyment of, and enthusiasm for, learning? What happens? What gets in the way?

The pressures of education and work mean that life can be stressful and demanding. As children become aware of the judgement of others they develop beliefs which lead to habits that will help or hinder their future as learners. Suddenly the frustrations that we inevitably experience as learners – making mistakes, getting it wrong, falling down – are witnessed, and judged, by others around us. Our teachers and classmates can see, and give us feedback: 'Well done, Jemmy, a good try', 'You got that wrong', 'What a nice picture', 'You speak funny', 'I choose you for my team', 'You need to work harder', 'I don't want to be your friend', 'Can you catch this?', 'Make your numbers clearer', 'Think of a better story', 'That's the wrong answer', 'Speak up', 'Be good'. And so it goes, endlessly.

In this way, we develop a view of the world and of ourselves which creates a framework of values and beliefs about our potential to be successful in life. Children and adults are exquisitely sensitive to the feedback they get. Praise can become addictive, and we strive to get more of it. On the other hand, criticism can feed doubts about our self-efficacy which linger in our unconscious and put limits on what we are willing to do – unless we reframe the criticism and see it instead as useful feedback, which can help us along the path to mastery. It's this feedback that has an influence right from the start of life.

When I was at school I didn't even really think that what I was doing *was* learning. It just felt like trying to remember stuff for exams and trying to avoid getting it wrong. I now feel as if all the valuable stuff I have learned has happened since leaving school and going to work.

Many of us don't consider ourselves to be great learners. Learning that is associated with exams and testing, being judged and experiencing failure, skews the way we perceive it. Instead of perceiving learning as 'growing', we often begin to think of learning as a method by which we, and others, judge our intelligence and self-worth. If we can reframe that thinking so that learning comes to mean exponential discovery and exciting personal development, it suddenly becomes more attractive and engaging. Put simply, learning will then become the lifelong project of growing your brain.

Children also become adept at picking up on social hierarchies, and soon learn the pecking order of the groups they are in. And these distinctions get more powerful the older children get. Eventually, learning isn't as important as appearing cool or streetwise and fitting in.

Our education system and the process of growing up can mean we lose touch with our inner baby and being learners for life. We become so used to comparing ourselves with other people that we forget that *real* growth is about our own journey and development. Instead of thinking, 'She's more knowledgeable, clever, successful than I am', it's more profitable to think in terms of how you are growing and changing. Do you ask how *you* are doing? What progress have you made compared to yesterday or last week? Are you more knowledgeable, clever and successful now? And do you ask where you need to direct your attention so you can take steps towards becoming who you want to be?

Think of the last time you proactively learned something. Maybe you cooked something new, using unfamiliar ingredients, or learned how to use your new mobile phone or tablet. Perhaps someone taught you how to play chords on the guitar or solve a computer problem. Was it easy or frustrating? Did you feel like giving up at times? What made you stick at it? When you cracked it, how did that feel? Did you want to do more? What really motivated you to grow that particular new neural pathway? Was it to impress someone else, or was it because you love to challenge yourself?

Growing your mindset using metacognition

If we all could focus on choosing to grow and develop a better mindset for life, maybe we could live in a happier, healthier and more successful society and feel better about ourselves. To be able to do this, we need to stand back from our thoughts and emotions, examine them, and be able to understand and change them.

For this process of metacognition (meta = outside, higher order, cognition = thinking), the starting point is to reflect and read. Many books have been written on how to become a better person. I've read lots of them. I've been on courses, done training sessions, and have become a better person as a result. So what I can offer you in the following chapters is not some amazing secret, but simply an account of my own experience, combined with a great deal of common sense, presented in a practical, pragmatic way. I hope it will be useful to you.

Reflect and review

- Choosing to grow means being willing to grow new neural pathways by learning new things and challenging our comfort zones.
- Choosing to grow and learn is a natural instinct in all of us from the day we were born.
- As we grow up and encounter challenges in life, we start to worry about what others think of us, instead of focusing on our own growth.
- Being able to keep growing means managing our thinking so that when times are tough we have some positive mantras and self-talk to steer us back on course.
- Developing a growth mindset means privileging learning, and believing that intelligence can be developed through effort.
- Learning comes from challenging ideas you may have about

yourself, and constantly seeking out strategies to improve – which are right for you *at this time*.

- People are different, and they all do things for their own reasons, based on their understanding of how the world works.
- Understanding how your thinking is affected by your emotions gives you more flexibility and self-control.
- Many books and theories have been written about success and happiness: the secret is to find out what works for *you* – and use it.

By reading this, you could have just grown a new neural pathway! When you learn something new your brain connects it to what it already knows thereby extending your neural networks.

Points of view

Q I have read many books on positive thinking and been on several courses on the subject. I have come to the conclusion that the people who read these books and go on these courses are rather self-obsessed and naive. There always seems to be a new notion, from walking on hot coals to the current ridiculous obsession with staring at a blank sheet of paper – so-called mindfulness. I have concluded that all this hocus-pocus around personal development is a con. So I am of a mind to continue to be a grumpy middle-aged man – and enjoy being grumpy. Any advice?

A The fact that you have been willing to explore personal development through reading and courses shows that you do actually have some questions you want answered. Instead of judging the other people who attend courses, how about exploring what makes you interested in the subject, and thinking about how you can apply any of these notions to your own experiences.

It's hard not to be cynical sometimes when you see another theory bandwagon coming along, but I have found it best to just use what works for me. We don't have to embrace new ideas without critical appraisal, but suspending disbelief can sometimes open up possibilities. Does your description of yourself as 'grumpy' suggest you may want to occasionally throw off that feeling and try out being a happy middle-aged man?

Chapter 2

The human condition

Get some perspective!

'Each person's task in life is to become an increasingly better person.'

Tolstoy[1]

We all want to be confident and successful in the all-important areas of life such as school, work, family and community, but how many of us truly believe that we are *already* confident and successful? During my career, I have taught thousands of teenagers and subsequently trained thousands of teachers and leaders. In the process I've discovered the unsettling truth that even the most successful of us have a lot of self-doubt.

I once worked with a very successful head teacher. Not only did he lead an Outstanding school, but he was truly loved by his staff and his students because he was warm and clever and a very good leader. When I visited him to review his school's progress we hit it off very quickly, laughing and sharing family stories. He had just remarried and had much-loved grown-up daughters and grandchildren. His school was going from strength to strength, and we met up frequently over

1   L. Tolstoy, *Path of Life*, M. Cole (trs) (Hauppauge, NY: Nova Science Publishers, 2002 [1910]), p. 189.

the next year or two. He had big plans for new school buildings and for reviewing the curriculum. He cared very much for his learners. One day I shared with him a struggle I had experienced with a member of staff, and he admitted how tough and lonely it could be at the top. It was almost a throwaway reflective comment, which was quickly replaced by his usual warm smile and jovial banter. Some weeks later, I received a phone call to say he had committed suicide.

I was shocked, because nobody had had any indication he was depressed. How could this happen to someone who seemed, on the surface, to be so happy and successful? After all, he had been making great plans for the future.

Although we may appear successful to the outside world, what really matters is what is going on in our heads. What makes us happy or sad, strong or vulnerable? The internal dialogue that delivers the commentary on our life can be very powerful in either empowering or undermining us. This constant internal commentary both creates and continually modifies our view of the world. This suggests, then, that the first stage of really understanding ourselves – and one another – is to gain some understanding of how this internal commentary interacts with, and shapes, our lives.

It isn't what happens to us in life that matters. It is how we perceive it, make sense of it, and how we respond and react to it that moulds us. We can look in the mirror and see a fat person, when we are thin, or see an ugly person, when we are beautiful. This, in turn, will affect how we treat our bodies – in terms of what we put into them and how we try to alter them. We can be told we are a successful, much-loved leader, but inside we think it may all fall apart at any moment. For some people, the only way to escape their negative thoughts and self-beliefs is to indulge in alcohol or drugs or other damaging behaviours that give temporary relief.

> Modern man can know himself only in so far as he can become conscious of himself.
>
> Carl Jung[2]

Even people who find themselves achieving great success in work, who earn prizes, who have glittering careers, fame and fortune, can suffer from 'imposter syndrome'. Over the years I have met extremely talented men and women who inspire others but who have a niggling belief that they are nothing but a fraud. Somehow, no matter how clever they are or how hard they have worked, they feel like an imposter: that they don't deserve their success; that it's all been a big mistake – and that they may lose everything at any moment. This is why, for some people, climbing the ladder of success is so much more satisfying than actually sitting on the top rung. Getting there can mean waiting for someone else to climb up and push us off, saying, 'What on earth are *you* doing here?'

Your sense of perspective on your achievements is all-important. If you hold the view that, no matter where you are on the ladder, you are still learning, still improving and that there is still much more you can do, this could help you. If you let yourself think that the only way forward is to go down again, it will give rise to fear and a mentality of guarding your back. And that is not conducive to happiness. There can be nothing sadder than to fulfil your dreams and still feel unhappy. And, worse still, we all have a tendency to think it could all go horribly wrong at any minute.

---

2   C.G. Jung, *The Undiscovered Self* (Abingdon: Routledge Classics, 2002 [1958]), p. 57.

Let's hear it for being paranoid

Natural selection favours the paranoid? Why do we have this tendency to think the worst, dread being found wanting, and conjure up fears and anxiety from nowhere? Consider this:

- -

Many thousands of years ago, two of our ancestors were busy hunting together in the jungle when they heard a rustle nearby. One of them thought, 'That could be a tiger!' and he ran away very quickly. His friend laughed at him later, because it was only the wind.

The next day the same thing happened. The same man thought, 'That could be a tiger!' and he ran away again. His friend was about to laugh when out jumped a tiger…

Guess who survived to produce offspring?

The same sort of thing has happened a million times since then, down thousands of generations. We have descended from those who sensed danger and ran away – even if the danger didn't materialise. From this 'we learned to see faces in the clouds and portents in the stars, to see agency in randomness, because *natural selection favours the paranoid* … Even now we are wired to believe that unseen things are watching us.'[3]

- -

The legacy of this is for us to be automatically afraid of the unknown, or of anything that is different or unexpected. As has been well documented, bad news sells, so every day we are bombarded with stories of disaster and the evil perpetrated by our fellow man. These stories feed

- -

3   P. Watts, *Echopraxia* (London: Head of Zeus Ltd, 2015), p.181.

this natural paranoia, confirm the natural negative bias in our thinking, and lead to the view that 'it's a wicked, wicked world'.

With the advent of social media, we now have even more connection with the dark side of human nature. Internet trolls can pounce on a throwaway remark and can destroy a career in 140 characters. On the other hand, the lovely, caring tweets and Facebook messages that flood in when a sick child needs treatment get relatively little attention. Only occasionally do we see, or hear, in the media a story of altruistic human organ donation or the turnaround of a career criminal. Given this daily bombardment of negative news, it can be hard to sustain a positive view of the world we live in. And this is despite the fact that many of us are far better off in a material sense.

But the way we see the world is a matter of balancing the good and the bad. We have to make a choice. We can choose to be passive, and to react to events by thinking that they are beyond our control and surrender to our natural negativity, or we can be proactive, and look for the positive in what might seem awful. It is that choice which will determine our state of mind from day to day. However, it doesn't always feel like a choice.

Figure 2.1 gives you an insight into how you may see yourself and other people in this world. If your view is 'I'm OK. You're not OK,' you may believe that other people are out to get you, or are untrustworthy, and that somehow you're being cheated. Something is wrong and your tendency is to blame others. If you lose £10 it's because the world is against you or someone must have stolen it.

If your view is that 'You're OK. I'm not OK', then you believe you don't deserve for good things to happen to you, everyone else seems to have it so right and you have it completely wrong. If you lose £10, you think it's typical of your luck, and even if you find a £10 note you would fear that someone will accuse you of stealing it, or you feel guilty – rather than celebrating your luck.

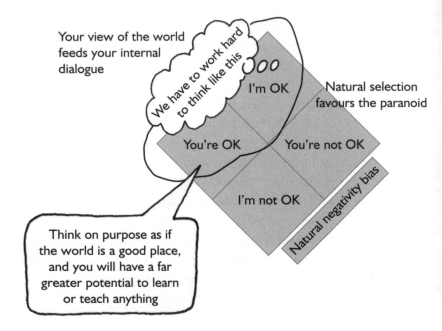

Figure 2.1: The OK corral.

However, if you believe the world is generally a good place, where positive things can, and do, happen, and if you see yourself as being a good person who tries to do the right thing, this will become the lens through which you judge and react to all of life's events. Basically you're thinking 'I'm OK. You're OK.' If this is how you see the world, then when things go wrong you will be less likely to blame yourself or others and will find a balanced, objective way to react to events. If you lose £10, you can be philosophical about it.

If you believe 'I'm not OK. You're not OK', then this book is definitely for you!

Can you reframe?

Reframing is a way of seeing things differently. Is that a snake on the path, or just a stick? Is your glass half-full or half-empty? Is that a threat or an opportunity? Having a natural tendency towards pessimism can make it very hard to see things in a positive way. Imagine it's raining on holiday – just like it always does. Your friend has let you down – again. Your work colleagues haven't met their deadlines, and that makes more work for you. You have a parking ticket, and you were only five minutes late back to your car! That bargain gift you bought has now been discounted by another 20%. Somebody else got the job, man, face, body, car, house you wanted – it's 'typical!'

There is no doubt that plenty of irritating stuff happens every day. Tragic, scary events can change your life in a moment: a huge loss in an investment. A phone call with some bad news about your health. The unexpected – or even expected – loss of a loved one.

These things will happen to all of us at some time. So how will *you* cope? Sometimes we see other people struggling with seemingly insurmountable challenges, such as looking after sick children or parents with Alzheimer's, or coping with a profound disability. How do many of these people stay relentlessly cheerful, despite their circumstances? You may think 'I couldn't ever do that, or be like that' – and then something bad happens to you and you *do* learn to cope, and even learn to see the positive side.

Conversely, some people find it hard to be cheerful and upbeat, even when they seem to have comparatively privileged or easy lives. Seeing things in a positive way is a lifelong challenge. I was recently in a supermarket on a gorgeous sunny day. Making conversation at the till with the cashier, I sympathised with her over her long shift and being stuck inside on such a day. Her reply was unexpected: 'Yes, it's gorgeous out there,' she said, 'but I'm near the door, so I can see the sun and I'm happy. It's the only way to be.'

Taking an interest in her positive mood, I enquired about her colleagues, because I'd noticed before how happy and enthusiastic the cashiers in this shop always seemed to be, despite the pressure to get people through the checkouts as fast as possible.

'Thanks,' she said. 'We all reckon you have a choice, and we like to keep each other cheerful with a bit of banter and an appreciation for having a job. There are far worse places to be in the world.'

How refreshing – and unusual. I left, a smile on my face, thinking, 'I'll return here to shop every week.'

Random acts of kindness change the world.

Whether you are coping with life's daily irritations or major life upsets, it may help to practise reframing. It may only take a slight alteration to your mindset to be able to find an alternative meaning. To practise, look at Figure 2.2 and see if you can find the two different images within each one.

Figure 2.2: Change your focus to see different pictures.

The brain first finds patterns in what it is seeing, then creates meaning. Notice how you can flip from one image to the other – and that you can't see both simultaneously, but only one image at a time. Maybe you see the young woman, then you look a slightly different way and see the old lady. Can you see the candlestick and the profiles in the next picture? These examples demonstrate how quickly the brain can adjust to make a new meaning or interpretation from the same basic input.

While we are thinking about the amazing ways our brains work, see if you can read this text:

I cdnuolt blveiee that I cluod aucalclty uesdnatnrd what I was rdanieg. The phaonmneal pweor of the hmuan mnid, aoccdrnig to a rscheearch at Cmabrigde Uinervtisy, it dseno't mtaetr in what oerdr the ltteeres in a word are, the olny iproamtnt tihng is that the frsit and last ltteer be in the rghit pclae. The rset can be a taotl mses and you can still raed it whotuit a pboerlm. This is bcuseae the huamn mnid deos not raed ervey lteter by istlef, but the word as a wlohe. Azanmig!

To have a go at this yourself, have a look at: www.leapbeyond.com/ric/scrambler/:

Our barnis hvae the caapicty to cosnrtuct maennig form any stiumlus. The aobve exmalpes are facsnitaing and hlep rmeind us to sotp and rfelcet on how we are seieng tihgns. Is tehre aontehr way of looikng at a siuttaion? Can we rerfmae it and mkae soemhting hvae a betetr otuocme tahn exepcetd? Tehre is reesrach evdience taht if we can hlep vunlrebale yuong pepole who fnid it hrad to laern to satnd bcak and rfeclet and sefl-erugalte tehy wlil ipmorve tehir prgoerss and inetlilegcne.

Or to put it another way:

Our brains have the capacity to construct meaning from any stimulus. The above examples are fascinating and help remind us to stop and reflect on how we are seeing things. Is there another way of looking at a situation? Can we reframe it and make something have a better outcome than expected? There is research evidence[4] that if we can help vulnerable young people who find it hard to learn to stand back and reflect and self-regulate, they will improve their progress and intelligence.

Thinking on purpose

Self-regulation requires us to be able to distance ourselves from our immediate emotional reaction to something and then reframe our thinking in order to control impulses. This is part of the process which I earlier called 'thinking on purpose' (or metacognition). It helps you manage your thinking to get the best outcome possible. We can all benefit from using metacognition. It encourages us to pause and

---

4   S. Higgins et al., The Sutton Trust - Education Endowment Foundation Teaching and Learning Toolkit (London: Education Endowment Foundation, 2014). Available at: https://educationendowmentfoundation.org.uk/evidence/teaching-learning-toolkit/meta-cognition-and-self-regulation/.

reflect – rather than be carried along in the never-ending river of 'important business', finding ourselves washed up somewhere we don't want to be.

Instead of simply reacting to circumstances and events, we stop, step back, think about and reframe events so that we deliberately take control and think in a new way. This is an essential habit if we want to use our experiences, good and bad, to help us grow stronger and wiser.

Many self-help books suggest variations on this theme. In Stephen Covey's *The 7 Habits of Highly Successful People* (1989), habit number one is 'Be proactive'. He talks of having *response-ability*: the ability to respond to events so that you don't become a victim or a martyr. You don't blame others when things go wrong, or define yourself as unlucky or hopeless. Instead, you should have a perspective that helps you respond to events – good or bad – in ways that grow your resilience.

It is this response-ability we should be trying to grow in each other by giving very specific, honest feedback. We soon find out at school that getting it right feels good and raises your self-esteem, but that getting it wrong hurts. However, if you can get in the habit of thinking that making mistakes helps you learn, you can apply the adage that there is no such thing as failure, *all* experience is feedback. This can help you find a way to move forward, rather than allowing setbacks to sink you.

That inner baby we discussed earlier had no such fear of getting it wrong. But peer pressure builds as we grow older, and we increasingly want to compare ourselves to, and impress, others. Sibling rivalry, friends who get more treats, classmates who have more friends – all of these rouse negative emotions that can grow. The following story is based on an ancient Cherokee legend, but its message is still true today.

Once upon a time there were two brothers who were part of a happy family living in a lovely home. Unfortunately, the brothers often quarrelled and bickered with each other. Eventually their parents lost patience and sent one of the brothers away for a few days to speak with his wise grandfather.

'I love my brother, Grandad, but sometimes I can't help hating him. He's too clever and bossy and everyone likes him more than me ...'

'I know just how you feel,' the grandfather replied. 'There is a fight going inside me too. It has been raging since I was your age, and it is between two wolves. One wolf is full of anger, envy, regret, greed, arrogance, self-pity, guilt, resentment, inferiority, lies, false pride, superiority and vanity. The other wolf is full of joy, peace, love, hope, serenity, humility, kindness, benevolence, empathy, generosity, gratitude, learning and compassion! These wolves are fighting within you – and inside every person – every day.'

The grandson thought about this for a minute and then asked his grandfather, 'Which wolf will win?'

The grandfather replied simply: 'The wolf you feed.'

Some people choose to feed only one of the two wolves, and so choose to live their lives at one end of the continuum shown in Figure 2.4.

For them, anger or love becomes a habit or default setting, often without them even realising it. Most of us, however, swing back and forth daily in this continuum of emotions and reactions. We give little thought to regulating our moods and emotions. As a result, we act impulsively, inconsistently and sometimes irrationally.

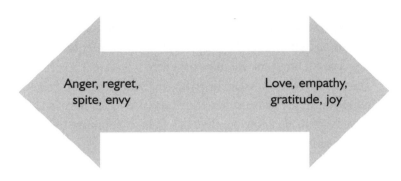

Anger, regret, spite, envy

Love, empathy, gratitude, joy

Figure 2.4: The continuum of emotions.

The solution to this is metacognition: the ability to stop, stand back, and pay attention to which direction your thinking is going in and why. You can then decide to think on purpose – to think differently, if what you are doing isn't getting you what you want.

Take a moment to consider where you are at the moment on this continuum – and why! Are you thinking on purpose, or accidentally feeding the big bad wolf?

Our natural negativity bias can kick in when we don't take time to understand or control our emotions. A throwaway comment from someone about our looks or actions can initiate a train of destructive inner dialogue that feeds on itself, creating misery and even physical symptoms such as nausea. Have you ever been emotionally hijacked like this? You might have been out with friends when someone made a sarcastic comment about you, or you felt ostracised by your friends when you came back from the bar to find you had nowhere to sit and that no one seemed to care. Perhaps, in the office, you worked hard on a plan with someone but during the presentation they seemed to get more credit and dominate the limelight.

You always have a choice about how to react if you stand back from your emotions and think on purpose, to reach a more positive outcome. In the work example above, you could think about what you learned about how your colleague performed, be glad for him or her, and think about how you will shine next time.

You have a choice. You can build up envy and bitterness, or gratitude and empathy. The battle between the wolves takes place in all of us. If we continually allow negative thoughts to dominate they will impact on and eventually change our beliefs.

Knowing your own darkness is the best method for dealing with the darknesses of other people.

Carl Jung[5]

Believe in the good

Metacognition requires us to look into our unconscious mind and investigate our beliefs. Consider Figure 2.5. What other people see of us – our attitudes and behaviours – is just the tip of the iceberg. At the base of the pyramid are our fundamental beliefs and values. Beliefs, including self-beliefs, are statements that you think are real and true (e.g. that God exists, that everyone is created equal, that you are happy and successful – or not!). One of my fundamental beliefs is that learning is the key to success and happiness. Lots of people use their beliefs as anchors or touchstones for decision-making in an otherwise uncertain world. Beliefs grow from what we are told, see, experience and read, and also our internal dialogue. Remember, what you regularly think is what you end up believing!

---

5   C.G. Jung, *C.G. Jung Letters: Volume 1 1906–1950*, G. Adler and A. Jaffé (eds), R.F.C. Hull (trs) (Abingdon: Routledge, 2015 [1973]), p. 237.

From these beliefs we develop our values – ideals we think are important and that can help people to know right from wrong. They can be described using words such as passion, resilience, selflessness, mastery, motivation amongst others (see p. 76).[6] Values describe, and provide a means of talking about, what is important to us.

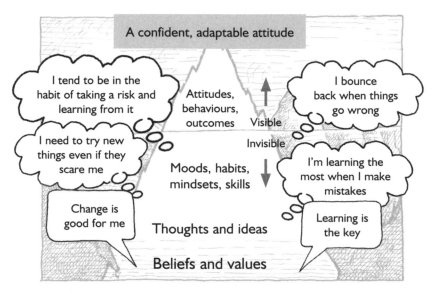

Figure 2.5: The belief pyramid.

Beliefs and values permeate our unconscious mind and influence our thoughts and ideas. For example, I believe in exercise: that it will make me healthy and feel good, so I value and desire fitness. This feeds up into my thoughts: 'I've been at this computer for hours; I need to take a walk. It will do me good.' Taking a walk regularly can then become a habit – especially now I have a pedometer that nudges me to do 10,000 steps a day! The outcomes from this habit are a healthier body

---

6   A full list can be found at: http://liveboldandbloom.com/05/values/list-of-values.

and mind – and walking every day also lifts my mood! In contrast, my husband believed it was best to unwind after work. So he valued rest and relaxation and thought a good way to achieve this was to chill out. Consequently, his habit was to lie on the sofa, channel-surf and snooze. His attitude to exercise after work and his behaviour were set – but the outcome was an expanding waistline. However, fortunately people can change their minds.

Our beliefs and values and the thoughts they lead to can be helpful and constructive, but they can also be negative and limiting. People with negative beliefs tend to have negative thoughts, along the lines of 'You're not OK.' This can lead to a lack of trust in others, so if a friend asks for a favour, the answer is likely to be no. People with a negative self-belief tend to think 'I'm not OK.' As a result, they have disempowering thoughts such as 'I can't …' or 'I won't be able to …' Thinking on purpose – practising metacognition and examining these thoughts when they surface – may be helpful.

Thinking on purpose

You may recognise some of the examples above – either in yourself or in others you work with or live with. Events trigger thoughts based on deeply seated, often unconscious, beliefs and values, which connect to feelings and lead to kneejerk reactions. To stop yourself being overwhelmed by your emotions, you need to take time to stand back, think about, and recognise what's happening. Take time to think about whether it is possible to reframe events. Think about and question your beliefs, thoughts, intentions, and kneejerk responses … and manage them.

Strong, positive beliefs and values protect us from being hijacked by our instinctive emotions because they help us rationalise and challenge our first reactions. Steve Peters, in *The Chimp Paradox*,[7]

---

7   S. Peters, *The Chimp Paradox* (London: Vermilion, 2012).

encourages his readers to create a Stone of Life to remind them of the core values they would like to have drive their lives. This helps you stand back and think on purpose about how your next steps can be congruent with your values. This means you feel comfortable with what you do because you believe it is fair and right. For example, if your job entails selling products to vulnerable people that they don't really need, this may clash with your core value of honesty. If you are not congruent with your values in your everyday life it can cause stress and anxiety. Chapters 5 and 9 give more detail on the importance of beliefs, and some activities you can try.

If we can become aware of how our beliefs and values are influencing our thinking, we can take more control of our emotions and get the outcomes we want. Being able to do this means we accept our thoughts as theories to be considered and evaluated. In this way, we can take time out and avoid the classic thinking errors, such as catastrophic thinking, which can involve imagining disastrous outcomes that never actually happen.

'Awfulising' and spotlights

Albert Ellis describes this type of irrational thought process as 'awfulising'.[8] It is a kind of negative exaggeration in which the way you think about and describe events or situations makes a minor setback seem like a major catastrophe or a fear even more real or terrifying.

Imagine someone pushes past you in a queue, someone insults your child, a dog poos in your garden, your washing machine packs up, or you fail to win the promotion you wanted. Suddenly you're thinking things like: 'Absolutely outrageous,' 'Downright disgusting,'

---

8 Catastrophic thinking was first described by Albert Ellis, founder of Rational Emotive Behavior Therapy, as one of his 'irrational' thought processes (#4). See www.rebtnetwork.org/library/ideas.html for more information.

'Typical!' 'It always happens to me,' 'I'm always getting it wrong.' For people with a negative thought bias, doing this helps 'prove' how wicked the world is and sets into motion a chain of thoughts, feelings and actions which can become self-fulfilling. The mere expectation that things will get worse will *cause* them to get worse.

If your partner is late arriving home, catastrophic thinking makes you think they have been in a car crash. So how do you respond when they do turn up? You may be angry, blame them for being late, or give them advice on time management, which is probably useless. Or you can be pleased to see them, because they are right here, now. It's your choice!

If we make a mistake at work or say the wrong thing in a meeting, our minds immediately leap ahead to the inevitable end of our career. Someone posts an unflattering, drunken picture of us on Facebook and we think that all our contacts will look at it and laugh at us forever. The truth is, it's unlikely anyone else will really care or notice. Being able to tweak your first response and choose a different, more positive way to look at the situation will give you more resilience. Worrying about what other people say or think can be a huge waste of energy!

This is particularly true in view of a phenomenon called the 'spotlight effect'. This refers to our tendency to overestimate how much attention other people are paying to us. Our own actions and words, embarrassing faux pas, disastrous mistakes and that big red spot on our chin often loom large in our own perception. But our perceived deficiencies are often not even noticed by others. It is our own thinking that shines the spotlight on ourselves.

A paper by Tom Gilovich and colleagues published in 2000 in the *Journal of Personality and Social Psychology* demonstrated this phenomenon empirically.[9] Groups of students were asked to complete an

---

9   T. Gilovich et al., 'The Spotlight Effect in Social Judgment: An Egocentric Bias
    in Estimates of the Salience of One's Own Actions and Appearance', *Journal of
    Personality and Social Psychology* (2000), 78 (2): 211–222.

unrelated task in the same room. One of the group was chosen to wear an embarrassing Barry Manilow T-shirt. The researchers asked those wearing the T-shirt to guess the percentage of other students in the room who could identify the person featured on the T-shirt. They guessed around 50% would identify Barry Manilow but, in reality, only 25% did.

They followed up this first set of studies with another where they tested whether the spotlight effect extends not just to people's appearances, but also their actions. They asked people to give a talk, and later recall their most embarrassing moments during it. Again, the study showed that the audience paid much less attention to any errors than the person delivering the talk did.

How would it change your confidence if you reminded yourself that nobody noticed the cringeworthy comment you made, or remembered that you spilled coffee all over yourself last week? And what about if you thought that even if they *had* noticed, they've now forgotten about it because they're worrying about their own bad hair day!

Another thinking trap we can fall into is black-and-white thinking: 'If I can't do it my way, I'm not going to do it at all,' 'If you don't love me, you must hate me,' 'If our relationship isn't loving today, it must be the end for us.' This type of thinking suits proactive types who want to take action as soon as they feel things aren't going well. The temptation is to solve the problem by taking immediate control and doing something. Sure, packing up and leaving your partner or job is one option, but it is only one option – so rein yourself in. Ensure the best available decision is being made, rather than suffer a future full of the unintended consequences resulting from black-and-white thinking. Pausing and thinking through the consequences of a variety of actions in a calm, logical way will usually create a better outcome.

Pause, reflect and reframe

Treating your thoughts as theories rather than facts helps you to create distance between your initial reaction to events and a carefully considered course of action. However, this is hard, because thoughts can create strong feelings. Getting in the habit of using metacognition to separate your thinking from your feelings will help worriers, perfectionists and those with low self-confidence. If you can deliberately stand back from your initial reaction by pressing the pause button and considering tweaking your reaction by thinking about it in a different way, you may be able to prevent those destructive emotions taking over.

It is a lifestyle choice to manage your thinking just as you might manage your physical fitness or financial wellbeing. In Chapter 6 we will consider in more detail how to manage our thinking to become more relaxed and happy.

Creating your own reality

When people are faced with the option of changing their minds or of finding new evidence so that they can keep their opinion, they will choose to look for new evidence rather than change their minds.

J.K. Galbraith[10]

10 Quoted in P. E. Merlevede et al., 7 Steps to Emotional Intelligence (Carmarthen: Crown House Publishing, 2000), p. 17.

The map is not the territory: this metaphor attempts to show how people can see the world in very different ways. It was originally used in 1933 by Korzybski[11] as the idea that we operate from mental maps that help us make sense of what we experience. People act from their own personal map of the world (as opposed to acting from 'reality'). Often we create and continually modify our map of reality. For example, Charlie had completely convinced himself he was a people person who was a natural team leader. But his arrogant, blasé style often made his colleagues squirm and sometimes even laugh behind his back when they heard him on the phone. He often took credit when sales were up, even if it wasn't due to his efforts. Unless a new strategy was his idea, he dismissed it, and he rarely followed through with promises made in team meetings to work with others. When he was made redundant he was told that feedback from his team suggested he needed to listen more and work collaboratively.

This feedback didn't fit with his 'map' because he was convinced he got on well with everyone. He decided that the mainly female team had problems working with a man and so the feedback was unjust. By the time he started his next job, he was thinking that it was professional jealousy of his sales skills that had led to him losing his previous job. Charlie was subtly recreating the past to fit his own preferred perceptions. No learning had taken place, so he would make the same mistakes again in his new job. He had made the territory fit his mental map of the world.

We all do this at times. It is a useful self-protection device to believe our own lies. Have you ever met someone who seems to have done everything you've done, but better? Their conversation is full of stories of extreme sports or encounters with danger or celebrities. They are convincing because they believe their own stories, but after a

---

11 A. Korzybski, *Science and Sanity* (Lakeville, CN: Institute of General Semantics, 1933).

while everyone else becomes a little sceptical. In conversation, we all recall and replay our experiences, but some people get into the habit of exaggerating – and sometimes don't even know they're doing it! Their stories become their map of the world. When someone else describes the same event, it may conflict with their recollection: 'Hmm, that's not the way I saw it …' – same event, different response … different outcome. We all filter the world through our own lens of beliefs and values. Look at these two genuine reactions to a first meeting of a women's action group:

'Everyone seemed so hostile and cliquey. I felt very self-conscious and a bit embarrassed to be there.'
'Everyone was smiling and happy, chatting away about what we could do as a group in the future.'

Brain scans can now show how the brain can filter information according to mood and habits. In a BBC *Horizon* television programme in 2013, the self-confessed anxious pessimist (and doctor) Michael Mosley was shown pictures of many different faces. He had to press a button on the computer each time he saw a happy face. On the first run-through, he missed many happy faces as he scanned the pictures. You can try a similar experiment yourself by following the link in the footnote.[12] Next, he took part in various activities aimed at getting him to understand his pessimistic thinking habits and change them, to give him a more positive state of mind.

The most powerful method for changing his mood proved to be mindfulness meditation – the opportunity to focus on his breathing and still his mind on a regular basis (see Chapter 9 for some ideas for

---

12 www.rainybrainsunnybrain.com/bbc-horizon/

how to make this part of your daily routine). These attempts at 'cognitive bias modification' (or engineered cheering-up) changed his brain activity so that his left and right brain activity were more in balance. People who tend to be pessimistic have greater activity on the right side of their brain than on the left – Mosley's brain became more equalised after the experiment. When he returned to the lab to try the experiment again with a similar set of faces, he spotted many more of the happy faces. By the end of the experiment Mosley had a better understanding of his own thinking, and could purposely pick out the happy faces.

When you look at a crowd do you see the happy or miserable faces? Can you adjust how you look at the world and see it differently if you want to?

Figure 2.6: Faces in a crowd.

The trouble is, we are all resistant to changing our perspective. Sometimes we don't even know how we are distorting things. Our maps of the world get adjusted as we grow and change. What is challenging is becoming familiar with other people's maps – because they are changing constantly as well. And mind-reading is difficult! It takes effort to understand someone else, so we rely on shortcuts – stereotypes, superficial cues – which generally work well. Sometimes, however, they don't, because the devil is in the detail. It isn't always helpful to categorise all homeless people as lazy or all bankers as thieves! I'm blonde and a bit scatty, but I can prove I'm not dumb.

You probably have a different viewpoint from your friend or partner about death or God or spicy curry. You listen and nod when they tell you their opinion, but you don't really get it. Sometimes it can actually make you angry that they just don't get your side of the argument. The presupposition in the metaphor 'the map is not the territory' is that there is no one 'real' map of reality; all we can ever have is our own version of reality. We may agree to respect different points of view and try to understand them. That's what makes life interesting, and maintains our curiosity, and is why reality TV shows are so popular: they pander to our insatiable voyeuristic desire to temporarily enter someone else's experience.

In real life we have to tread carefully, react to the cues the other person gives us, and adjust our behaviour to suit the occasion. We always need to remember that the meaning of our communication is the response we get. Whatever you meant to say, what really matters is the reaction it created. The comment 'You look tired' may have a caring intention behind it, but may be received as an insult. Praising someone's effort may be interpreted as patronising. We need to look out for the other person's reaction so we can adjust the message we are giving, to make sure what we say (and the way we say it) is having the desired impact. When we have a real rapport with someone, we can come to an understanding of what it means to say 'Every behaviour has a positive intention'[13] because we begin to understand other people's logic, reasoning and underpinning values. And these are different from our own.

This can mean that one person's reality or truth is another person's fantasy or lies. One person's terrorist is another person's freedom fighter. One person's fair comment is another person's malice. Making the switch is an example of reframing. Reframing can often be done simply by changing the language in our internal dialogue. By doing this we will create different responses. 'Mistake' becomes 'lesson', 'ending' becomes 'new beginning', 'threat' becomes 'challenge'. A different interpretation of events gives us more choice about how to respond, so it's good to keep your map flexible.

We all mentally rehearse every aspect of our lives – from vital interviews to mundane meetings, from big presentations to small conversations – even though we may not be aware we're doing it. We imagine what will happen, so we can then be prepared for it. Even though we know what we would *like* to happen, we rehearse all the possibilities, good and bad. These mental rehearsals are set on the stage created by our existing 'map of the world'. The stage can be either scary or exciting, colourful or gloomy. You decide! By adjusting the stage and thereby the context for our actions, we increase our chances of success – or failure.

Adjusting your map to get the best results

You are planning to go to an important meeting, but you aren't looking forward to it. You expect some people there will undermine you by ignoring your points, or will try to take credit for your ideas. You

---

13 'Every behaviour has a positive intention' is one of the presuppositions of neurolinguistic programming. See J. O'Connor and J. Seymour, *Introducing NLP* (San Francisco, CA: Thorsons, 1990), p. 131.

mentally rehearse the event for days, imagining your own and the other people's body language. You see yourself looking uncomfortable as you summon up the courage to offer your contribution. You see the conspiratorial looks they share with each other while you're speaking. You see their eyes roll as you present your argument. You feel the pressure of the awkward silences and hear your own thoughts bouncing around your brain: 'So unfair', 'I'm rubbish', 'They don't respect me', 'Smug know-alls', 'What chance have I got?'

The map of the world you have constructed in your mind predicts the outcome. On the day, you tentatively sidle into the meeting and sit quietly, building up nervous anxiety, your heart beating faster and your mouth dry until it's your turn to speak. Then you speak hesitantly and mumble and rush through your points. You have sabotaged your chance to make a good impression.

How about creating a different map of the world for this meeting? Mentally rehearse it so that you see yourself relaxed and enjoying the meeting. You are sure of your message and the important points within it. You're standing tall and looking confident. In your mind's eye, you shrink the picture of your colleagues so that they lose their dominance. You see yourself shine as you communicate, smiling with self-assurance and a hint of charisma. The words bouncing around in your head are 'clarity', 'rapport', 'determination', 'powerful message' and 'confidence'.

This reframing is never an easy task when the stakes are high, especially when anxiety and self-doubt are present. The good news is that, the more you practise, the easier it gets and the better you will perform.

Other people have maps too

Knowing how to understand and adjust your own map for the best results is important. But nothing will help you be more successful and popular than being able to tune in to other people's maps and see things the way other people see them. This is the secret of getting on with others.

You don't have to agree with other people all the time; you don't even have to like them or be their friend. But you do need to understand their viewpoint if you are going to communicate your ideas and influence them. As you know, it's unlikely that you will suddenly change their opinion, but you may be able to make them a little more open to your input, especially if they sense that you acknowledge and respect their perspective. As Stephen Covey explains in his seminal work on personal development, *The 7 Habits of Highly Effective People*, we need to try to understand other people before we can expect them to understand us.[14]

We all want to be understood and appreciated as the unique and special people we are. The secret is to put aside that need, and pay attention to the other person we are communicating with. This requires really intense listening, and letting them know you have a genuine interest in them; that your own views and needs come second. If you find yourself getting irritated or angry with their viewpoint or behaviour, you must control your emotions. This means you have to think on purpose – think as if you were looking through the eyes of the person you're speaking to, and imagine how their world works.

When you acknowledge and respect the different maps of the world of your colleagues, neighbours, friends or partner, you will

---

14 S. Covey, *The 7 Habits of Highly Effective People* (London: Simon & Schuster, 1989).

realise that they are all acting according to their own map and for their own reasons (though you may not agree with those reasons!). In this way you can step out of the cycle of judging and being judged, and make a satisfying emotional connection.

Beth's story

All my life I'd been fat – from a cute chubby baby to a stocky toddler. I made my own clothes as a young teenager because I couldn't find anything that fitted me in the fashion shops. I went to diet clubs, exercise classes, and aqua aerobics, and was frogmarched round my village as my family tried to slim me down so that I looked more like my tall, slim sister. I ate secretly in my bedroom – crisps and chocolates, mainly. It felt comforting to experience their lovely taste at the time, but I was filled with self-loathing afterwards.

For years my life seemed to revolve around resisting food and pretending to exercise. You have no idea how it feels to be a chubby person looking like they are trying to power-walk, or being the only fatty at the gym on the running machine. Family and friends were worried that I was just getting bigger and that I would soon be one of those people that need two seats on a plane. They either patronised me saying things like, 'Chubby people have more fun' or they gave me serious tough-love talk: 'You really need to think about healthy eating and losing weight' or 'You really need to take control before it's too late.' Take control … take control – don't you think I would have loved to be able to do that?

Then I met someone. Not a boyfriend, nor a lover, just someone who understood me – for the first time ever. We met while I was sitting on the village seat, out for a 'walk'. I was wondering if I could face applying for another job so I could get out of the local supermarket (where all the people like me seemed to work). I got upset thinking about having to face people's abuse or sympathy. He just sat down next to me and asked what was wrong.

'Nothing!' I said, trying to cover up my surprise and embarrassment.

He smiled and said, 'I'm just interested in what you're thinking,' and looked at me without sympathy or emotion, just genuine curiosity. It all tumbled out. My jealousy of my sister, my irritation about how my mum gave me small portions and left Weight Watchers brochures on my bedside table. About not getting picked for teams, finding small chairs uncomfortable. About people being obsessed by my weight, my body, my eating … That nobody really cared about *me* … It was only when I was saying it all that I realised how much there was to say.

It didn't change me straight away, but that night I didn't raid my chocolate store.

Someone had actually bothered to ask Beth how she felt. The first time she had someone who listened to her, she also listened to herself. She began to wrestle with her underlying beliefs and the reality of her situation. This helped her realise she was lying to herself, and helped her take the first step to controlling her habits. That first step is metacognition – Beth thinking about her thinking, in order to start changing it.

Everyone has their personal map of the world. Recognising how you see the world through your own eyes, then being able to see and understand the world through the eyes of the other person gives you the awareness you need to manage your own and understand other people's perspectives. To do this, you need the mental flexibility to stand back, think about how you are seeing things, and then be brave enough to attempt to adjust your picture to be more aligned to the results you want. For example, you want to start your own small business but you think this is just for people who are pushy and confident. In your world, people like you don't start a business, so if you want to achieve this, you will have to change the way you perceive your potential to grow the required skills and see opportunities rather than barriers. Doing this is a continuous challenge, because we often want to just dig in and do what we've always done, even if we are not particularly satisfied with our lives. Making a determined effort to be reflective and think more deliberately gives you choices.

The best way to get really good at this is to help others do the same by being a powerful influencer. Not by telling them what to think or do but by getting curious about what motivates them. This means you help your friends, family and colleagues to reflect on their thinking by asking coaching questions that help them think of new solutions or perspectives. There is much more to read about this in Chapters 7, 8 and 9.

Reflect and review

- Your view of the world is important, as it creates the frame through which you see everything.
- Many of us have a tendency to see and think the worst.
- So much of our thinking is fed by thoughts and beliefs that we are not even consciously aware of.

- Our mental map of the world is a powerful predictor of our success or failure, happiness or discontent.
- Metacognition helps us to think on purpose in a conscious way, instead of allowing our emotions to overrun our reason.
- Taking the time to listen and connect with someone else and explore their map of the world will help you improve your relationships at home and at work.

Points of view

Q I'm struggling to see the world as an OK place at the moment. War, terrorism and climate change are just some of the ways we humans are destroying the world. When I'm out I see people throwing litter out of their cars or swearing at their kids. There are more and more betting shops and fast-food outlets in the high streets, with obese families taking full advantage of the latter. There is massive want and poverty, and bankers and billionaires who are just out for themselves. I honestly am struggling to reframe this and try to see anything positive, so I wake up most days feeling quite gloomy and sad, despite having a good job and a lovely family. Any advice?

A Your letter certainly highlights some very negative aspects of life today. We read about all of this and see it on the news every day. And yet … think about your own life.

When was the last time someone said something nice to you or you helped someone else out? What do you like about your family and friends? Does anyone in your community organise litter picks or charity events? How much did people raise for Children in Need this year?

(Are the answers: Not that long ago. Lots of things. Yes. Millions!?)

What I'm trying to say is, although we see the bad and the tragedy around us, we mustn't let that block out the good stories and the small, everyday happy moments. By taking action, we can feel a little less disempowered by world events. Try raising money for your favourite charity or helping out at a homeless shelter. Carry out a random act of kindness. Yes, it may only be a drop in the ocean, but doing something, no matter how little, presents an alternative to feeling sad. Encourage others to join you. It's the first step to making a bigger difference and to feeling happier.

As far as we can discern, the sole purpose of human existence is to kindle a light in the darkness of mere being.

Carl Jung[15]

Q   I am passionate about personal and professional development, but sometimes find managing other people so frustrating. I was brought up to work hard, and know that success comes from effort and taking responsibility. I've worked very hard to achieve real success in my business life, but managing other people is a constant challenge. I now have people in my team who just will not admit when they have screwed up. They always have an excuse or someone else to blame. This often has a direct impact on meeting our targets but they don't seem to care.

I spend hours trying to coach these people into taking some responsibility, so that they can move forward, but they are stuck

15 C.G. Jung, *Memories, Dreams, Reflections*, A. Jaffé (ed), R. Winston and C. Winston (trs) (New York: Vintage, 1989 [1962]), p. 326.

and seem to get angry or upset, so we don't get anywhere. Then they expect a pay rise! I'm becoming disheartened, and am convinced some people just can't change.

A It's good to know that you have such a strong work ethic. It must have helped you get to your present position. Look again at your difficult team members. They will have some redeeming qualities, even if you have only seen in them in the past. List these. Also, have you tried focusing on the outcomes you want from this situation? Do you want every member of your team to take responsibility for the failure of the task rather than shift the blame? Do you want them to learn from this situation and thereby grow and change?

It is worth remembering, though, that people can only grow and change if they are allowed to make mistakes and feel confident about admitting to their mistakes because they feel they won't be judged. Have you ever made a mistake? What helped you admit to it and take responsibility? Who did you feel comfortable admitting it to? Was it a boss who knew that making mistakes was part of the learning process? Your passion for personal development has probably helped give you the confidence to face your mistakes and learn from them. Maybe others haven't learned that lesson … yet.

Does your success (or high standards) frighten people into taking a defensive stance and making excuses? Show your team that you also make mistakes and learn from them. Be the change you want to see. Create a culture that shares and celebrates learning from mistakes, rather than one which is simply about meeting targets. Of course, your priority will always be to deliver the bottom line, but getting your team to understand and share responsibility is your greatest challenge. To get the most out of people, try to see that from their point of view – they may be doing their best. And believe that anyone *can* change. If you can shift your thinking, you may be able to shift theirs.

II

Chapter 3

Know yourself

In this chapter you will be encouraged to take a long, hard look at yourself, as this is the starting point for being able to grow. There are a number of questions for you to answer and questionnaires to complete. They are designed to help you think on purpose and reflect on how you see yourself in relation to other people and the world in general. It is good to stand back and consider what you think, how you respond to situations, and what motivates you. Answer the questions and try the questionnaires – you may learn some surprising things about yourself.

I first filled in a self-analysis questionnaire during a training course for potential leaders. I was a part-time teacher in a large secondary school, and had two young children. At that time I used to gaze in awe at the leaders of large departments and our senior leadership team. They had experience and knowledge, could chair meetings, make decisions, inspire me by describing their vision … but most of all they got my respect because the buck stopped with them. When problems occurred, they had to take responsibility for them.

On this course we talked about our leadership skills and how to develop them. We role-played some mock interviews and filled out a self-assessment form about our potential to be a head teacher. I wasn't sure I had what it took, but I knew I was ready for some kind of change. The results from this extensive questionnaire were fed back to us some weeks later. To my absolute surprise, I was told that I had 98% of the skills and dispositions suited to headship, and was deemed to have a 'very high likelihood to succeed'. Of course, the feedback gave me a really nice feel-good factor but, much more importantly, it planted a seed in my head that maybe, one day, I too could be a leader. When I finally did become a leader in a junior role, I soon realised that those confident-looking people, who seemed so secure and decisive, had just as many insecurities as I did. And the very best ones – the ones I thought had and knew it all – admitted that, like me, they were still learning. This chapter aims to help you think about your potential.

Check yourself out

Have you tried out your mood monitor yet? Every copy of this book includes one, and it looks like Figure 3.1.

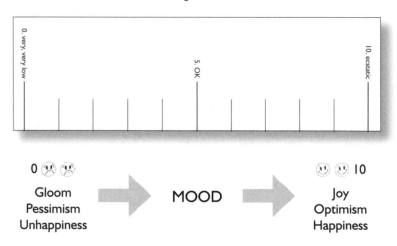

Figure 3.1: The mood monitor.

All you need is a paper clip to slide along it to the point which accords with how you feel. If you have started to use your mood monitor, you have started to understand how you think and feel. This chapter delves a little deeper into what makes you tick.

Taking notice of what puts you in a good mood (going for a walk, having a cuddle, eating chocolate, passing an exam, being out in the sunshine) and what puts you in a bad mood (queuing, emails, not getting enough sleep, sarcasm, worrying thoughts) can help you take control of, and understand, your thoughts and feelings.

Understanding how your moods work is the first step towards taking control of them. In order to grow, you need to know where you are. To do this, you need to reflect from time to time on important questions such as:

- What sort of mindset do I have?
- What is my default setting?
- Am I an optimist or a pessimist?
- How does this affect my mood?
- How does this affect my personal and professional relationships?

To answer these questions you need to be able to reflect on your thinking. It's not that you have to be permanently cheerful, but you may benefit from being able to recognise your habitual state of mind and adjust it if you want or need to.

Do you know your own default setting?

If you had to place yourself on the mood monitor continuum, where would you normally be? In other words, if you were having an ordinary day without any dramas or catastrophes, what is your default setting? Think of a number between 0 and 10 – and be honest!

Now think of people you know who are great to be around, who always fill you with energy, and seem to radiate optimism. Then think of others – the ones who seem to drain you, who always seem to see the glass as half-empty, and who spread gloom and despair. Do they know they are having this effect? Have you told them? Probably not – and for this reason it is very easy to be unaware of our own default setting – no one has told you!

It may well be worth asking colleagues, friends and family what they consider your default setting to be. When you communicate with them, do you inspire and cheer them up or do you spread contagious misery? Do they see you as a radiator, or are you an unwitting drain? It takes courage to ask for this sort of feedback – and courage to give it, so to start with you might prefer to try a different way of coming at this. You could use the mood monitor questionnaire in Table 3.1.

Table 3.1: The mood monitor questionnaire.

Answer the questions below by ticking one of the boxes from strongly agree to strongly disagree	Strongly agree	Agree	Mostly agree	Mostly disagree	Disagree	Strongly disagree
1 I wake up in the morning expecting to have a good day.						
2 I don't expect the people I meet today to improve my mood.						
3 I find that if I work hard and put the effort in things turn out well.						

Answer the questions below by ticking one of the boxes from strongly agree to strongly disagree	Strongly agree	Agree	Mostly agree	Mostly disagree	Disagree	Strongly disagree
4 When things irritate me, I find it hard to shake it off.						
5 I really enjoy the feeling of being stretched and challenged.						
6 I believe that, no matter how hard you work, someone could undermine your efforts.						
7 I sometimes find the success of others demotivates me because they don't always deserve it.						
8 I often try to find out from others how they see me so that I know how to improve.						
9 There are some things about myself that I just can't change.						
10 I enjoy tackling problems to see a project through to the end.						
11 I feel better about myself when I'm in my comfort zone and doing the things I'm used to.						
12 It is important that I have the opportunity to learn at work.						

After you have done this, work out your score by looking at the following mood monitor self-scoring chart. See which answers you gave to the mood monitor questions, and circle the number in the same box. Then add up the numbers and compare your score to the descriptions after the self-scoring chart.

Question number	Strongly agree	Agree	Mostly agree	Mostly disagree	Disagree	Strongly disagree
1	6	5	4	3	2	1
2	1	2	3	4	5	6
3	6	5	4	3	2	1
4	1	2	3	4	5	6
5	6	5	4	3	2	1
6	1	2	3	4	5	6
7	1	2	3	4	5	6
8	6	5	4	3	2	1
9	1	2	3	4	5	6
10	6	5	4	3	2	1
11	1	2	3	4	5	6
12	6	5	4	3	2	1

The higher your score, the more optimistic your default setting is:

51/72. You have a natural inclination to expect the best every day. This can put pressure on you, because sometimes things don't turn out well and you have to cope with the disappointment and still see this in a positive way. However, your optimism will often help things turn out well.

26/50 You have days when you can expect the very best of people and events but at times you can't help being a realist or thinking the worst. It is worth considering if there are some areas of your life that make you more optimistic than others: for example, work or family time. Then consider why this is, and how you can widen your positive expectations to all areas of your life. Notice how you frame your positive thoughts when you do this.

12/25. Your natural inclination is to take a pessimistic view. This may protect you from being disappointed if things don't turn out well, but it can also make you irritable and easily annoyed by the little things in life. Practise reframing some of your thoughts and see if that works for you. Also try meditating for five minutes every day (see p. 239).

Self-evaluation and seeking feedback

Do you self-evaluate? If so, do you find that there is nothing you need to do to be happier or to improve yourself and grow? If that is true, lucky you! Or are you, like everyone else who is honest with themselves, able to see that not everything is as good as it might be? Then what do you do as a result?

Are you good at *asking* for feedback? Are you good at *taking* feedback? Are you good at *acting* on feedback?

Many people don't ask for advice or feedback. There can be lots of reasons for this, but the most common ones are:

- *They are unaware that they might need to.* People like this may be in blissful ignorance of their faults – they are unconsciously incompetent. Getting feedback is not something that has occurred to them – yet! They have probably never self-evaluated or done so honestly.
- *They don't see the need to.* They are aware that it is possible to get feedback, but – arrogantly – do not think they need it. They have evaluated themselves and are happy to continue doing things as they have always done – even if what they are doing may be wrong.
- *They are too proud to.* This group may have self-evaluated and become aware that things are not going perfectly. They realise that feedback might be useful, but think that seeking it will somehow demean them – especially if they were to get feedback from someone close to or, worse still, junior to them.
- *They are afraid to.* This group really are self-aware insofar as they know that things are not going perfectly. They know that feedback could be useful, but they don't ask for it. This is either because they think that they might have to change as a result of the feedback (which frightens them), or that the feedback will be critical and they might not be able to respond to it, which might lead them to an even worse place.

Do you fall into any of the above categories, or do you ask for advice? As you read in Chapter 2, actively seeking feedback is a good sign. It shows you have a growth mindset, and is a prerequisite for personal growth.

How do you take feedback, once you have sought it? As criticism or as help? This, of course, depends on how the feedback is given. Some people are hopeless at giving feedback, making it sound like a litany of what you have been doing wrong and how it has affected them, rather than a constructive conversation about what you might do better and how it would benefit you.

The most effective feedback focuses on:

- what exactly you need to do to improve
- helping you take the steps towards improvement
- what improvement would look like for you after acting on the feedback.

If you do seek feedback, insist that it is given in this spirit. If you do, there is much more chance of a successful outcome because you feel ownership of the feedback – it is being done *with* you, not *to* you!

Being good at taking feedback doesn't mean that you will always do what other people suggest, but it does mean that you can listen to alternatives and objectively consider their value. Tapping into other people's experience and knowledge means you have a far greater chance of getting it right. It's obvious, isn't it?

Don't restrict taking advice or seeking feedback to the big decisions in life either, such as getting a new job, moving house or moving in with a partner. Have you always driven a certain make of car, or used a certain supermarket? Do you find, then, that when someone suggests alternatives, you automatically dig your heels in and reject their advice without considering it? Do you believe that *you* always know best? Do you resent or feel dismissive or cynical about other people's opinions?

This is how we can get trapped into doing what we have always done, because it feels comfortable and safe. Listening to advice or, even worse, being criticised, can prompt a negative emotional response that stops us from being flexible and adaptable. Reflect on your responses in the situations shown in Table 3.2.

Table 3.2: Change your response.

	Do you ...	Or do you ...
You are advised to consider changing your job by your boss.	Think that your boss sees you as a threat and feel angry and hurt. Consider reporting your boss for bullying and going to an employment tribunal.	Seek out a variety of opinions about your strengths and weaknesses from colleagues, customers and managers. Ask your boss about your strengths and what training might help you overcome any weaknesses.
A friend suggests you should lose weight to get healthy.	Stop talking to him or her, because who needs friends like that?	Measure your weight and height, find your body mass index (BMI) and compare this to the BMI charts for your age and sex. Then, if you're overweight, take advice about the best way to diet and get fit, and thank your friend for the hint.

	Do you …	Or do you …
Your family say they are irritated because you are always late.	Ignore them, because being late doesn't bother you as you always have other pressing things to do – and, anyway, you have so many other good points that you know people don't mind if you are late.	Reflect on when and why you are late. Ask friends to see if they agree with your family. If they do, make a plan to change the way you get ready to see them, so that you arrive extra early.
On a night out, a good friend suggests that your relationship with your partner doesn't seem to be going well at the moment.	Carry on as you are, as you can't risk losing the stability of your current home life. Avoid this friend in future.	Ask your friend why he or she feels like this, and reflect on it. Go home and talk to your partner about it to make a plan to improve things, and move on.

Figure 3.2 is helpful for self-evaluation. It is a model about self-disclosure called the Johari window.

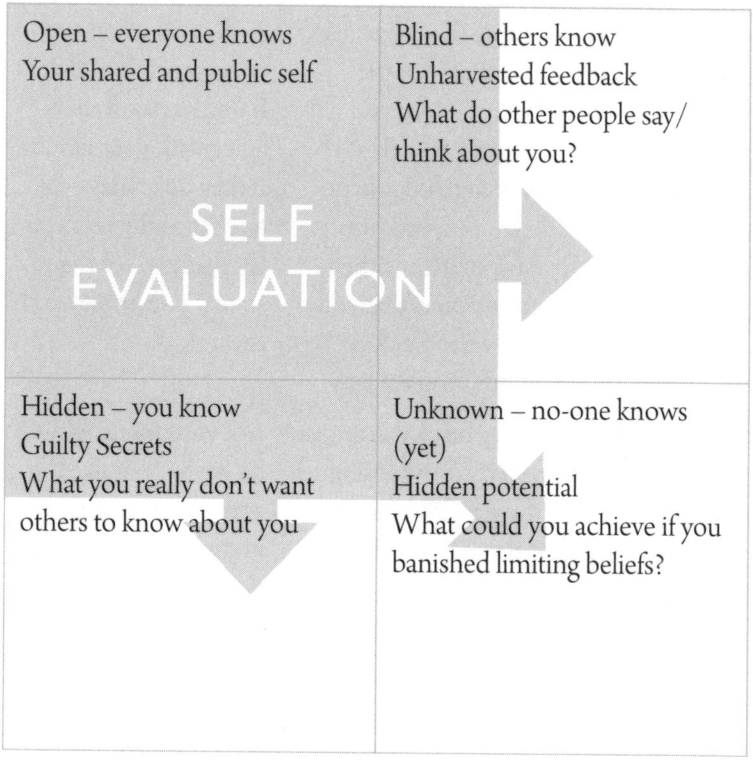

Open – everyone knows Your shared and public self SELF EVALUATION	Blind – others know Unharvested feedback What do other people say/ think about you?
Hidden – you know Guilty Secrets What you really don't want others to know about you	Unknown – no-one knows (yet) Hidden potential What could you achieve if you banished limiting beliefs?

Figure 3.2: The Johari window (adapted from J. Luft and H. Ingham, 1955).[1]

The 'Open' quadrant of the diagram represents your public persona. It contains information that everyone knows about you, such as your name, address, job and possibly hobbies and interests. It also includes

---

1   G. Burton and R. Dimbleby, *Between Ourselves: An Introduction to Interpersonal Communication* (New York, St Martin's Press, 1988), p. 38.

events and relationships which you share with the public on social media.

In the 'Blind' quadrant are things about you that other people notice but you don't know about. This may include your irritating habit of speaking too loudly in meetings, not buying a round in the pub, or your bad breath. People may talk about these things behind your back, but may be too embarrassed or too frightened to tell you about them face to face. What *do* other people say about you? It may be complimentary things like how caring or how positive you are, or how good your new makeup/hair/outfit looks. You won't find out what these things are, positive or negative, unless you ask people for their feedback.

Next is the 'Hidden' quadrant: the parts of you or your history which you like to keep secret. They may be fairly harmless things, such as bad habits or those cringingly embarrassing moments we all experience in life. More seriously, you may have a past which you want to hide or keep private, especially if you feel that sharing details could affect your future personal and working relationships. This could be a criminal record, past alcohol or drug abuse, adoption, or similar things. You may also have ongoing problems you want to keep secret, such as an eating disorder, self-harm or drug use. (The importance of disclosing problems like these is discussed in Chapter 6.)

The final quadrant is your 'Unknown' self: your untapped, unexplored potential or talents. So many of us discover as we go through life that, all along, we had hidden potential to write a book, learn a new skill, play golf, sing, lead an organisation, run a marathon, grow vegetables, swim the Channel, etc. Explore the 'Unknown' quadrant by saying 'Yes' to every new opportunity or challenge. This is risky – you may be going into unknown territory and think you may not be up to it. It takes courage to do this, and push yourself outside your comfort zone. But it is only when you are outside your comfort zone that you will discover your hidden potential and talents – and grow.

Look back at the Johari window. You will see that, to grow, you need to discover a little bit more at every opportunity about your 'Blind' quadrant through asking for feedback. You also need to communicate your thoughts and feelings and share more of your 'Hidden' quadrant to unburden yourself of guilty secrets and seek help. Finally, you need to try to take up new opportunities and to do something that scares you every day to discover more of your 'Unknown' self.

Get more feedback and push yourself outside your normal comfort zone on a regular basis. This is done through regular self-evaluation. The more you do of this, the further you will go in the direction of the arrows, and the more you will learn and know about yourself. Take a moment to plan how you will do this. Dangerous, even life-threatening, behaviours, like those mentioned at the end of the description of the 'Hidden' quadrant, can begin with simple thoughts of self-doubt and anxiety. Over time, if kept hidden, these thoughts can become magnified. This is because keeping worries inside your head leaves them unrestrained, unmonitored and not subject to the reality check and help that you might get if you shared the problem with others.

If no alternative viewpoint is being offered to your troubled mind, destructive thoughts will eventually influence your belief system. As I said earlier, what you regularly think is what you end up believing. In this way you really can end up believing these destructive thoughts. Thinking that you are fat, ugly, stupid, worthless, friendless and hopeless becomes self-reinforcing, and you spiral further downward. Eventually, even though you try to keep this as your guilty secret, it will impact on your behaviour or health. In time, other people will start to notice and express their concern.

The best way out of this trap is to bring your darkest, grimmest thoughts and worries out into the 'Open' quadrant early on and share them. Talking therapies such as counselling are successful because they give people a chance to share some of their 'Hidden' material in confidence and to step back and take an objective look at the effects of their thoughts and behaviour. Revealing, sharing and discussing problems gives a different perspective on them and can help lift a weight from your shoulders. This is why communication is such a priority for growth. Listening, talking and sharing what is inside your head increases your resilience as you are learning new perspectives every day. The more you share your map of the world with other people, the more they will have a chance to understand you, and the more they will trust you with their own 'Hidden' side.

Try acting as if ...

You might be asking yourself how it is possible to overcome the barriers preventing you from changing your default setting. Or you might be thinking that it may be just too hard for you to self-evaluate and explore the other three quadrants in the Johari window. Where will you get the courage from to get feedback, share secrets and explore the 'Hidden' quadrant?

Happily, these things are possible with a little practice at 'acting as if'. As the Dalai Lama said in *The Art of Happiness*: 'The systematic training of the mind – the cultivation of happiness, genuine inner transformation by deliberately selecting and focusing on positive mental states and challenging negative mental states – is possible because of the very structure and function of the brain.'[2]

Acting as if is all about focusing on positive mental states and *acting as if* you are the person you want to be. If your default setting is one which tends towards negativity in one or more aspects of your life, you can act as if you're positive. Acting as if is worth doing because it will make you a more open, flexible person, and will help you grow and

---

2 HH Dalai Lama and H.C. Cutler, *The Art of Happiness: A handbook for living* (London: Hodder, 1999), p. 29.

become happier in future.

For example, if you want to edge towards 10 on the mood monitor, try this experiment to begin with:

Recall what it feels like when you are happy. Identify the activities that make you happy, and visualise yourself doing them. Remember your emotions at those times. Did you smile more often, hear more acutely, walk differently, and feel differently towards others? Picture yourself immersed in those thoughts and feelings, and then begin to act as if that is how you are thinking and feeling now. See how it feels inside your head to act as if. Practise this, then try it out for real. Are you walking differently? Smiling more often? Feeling warmer towards others? Are you using different words with a friendlier intonation? Do you have different thoughts inside your head?

Afterwards, consider whether or not pretending to be happy changed your mood for the better. There is growing evidence that when you smile and laugh, your brain chemistry changes, and this can change the way we think:

'Smiling, for instance, tricks your brain into thinking you are happy so it starts producing the neurochemicals that actually do make you happy.'

Shawn Achor[3]

---

3   S. Achor, *The Happiness Advantage: The seven principles of positive psychology that fuel success and performance at work* (London: Virgin Books, 2010), p. 206.

Our brains are far more adaptable than we used to believe, and remain so throughout our lives. This flexibility is called neuroplasticity – the ability of the brain to lay down new neural pathways. It has been seen in all sorts of situations: for example, in recovering stroke patients, where the functions carried out by damaged parts of the brain are taken over by nearby undamaged areas and, less dramatically, in people learning a new language. Brain plasticity means that your personality and intelligence are not fixed, but have the capacity to grow and develop.

Just as repeated piano practice lays down strong neural pathways that result in seemingly effortless expertise, having the same responses to life's events lays down strong neural pathways that become habitual and hard to rewire. This is great if the habitual hardwired response is optimism, but not so great if the habitual hardwired response is pessimism or negative bias. But change is possible. The plasticity of our brain is no longer in dispute: our personality and intelligence are not fixed but are endlessly malleable. Your brain can, and will, change as a consequence of hard, purposeful work and repeated practice. You can change your default state, and repeatedly acting 'as if' is a powerful tool for doing so.

A crucial part of the future will be a recognition that a phenomenon like happiness is not a transient feeling or a fixed set point, but an *ability*. An ability that can be trained and developed and shaped.

Richard Davidson[4]

---

4 Quoted in L. Frank, *Mindfield: How brain science is changing our world* (Oxford: Oneworld Publications, 2007), p. 133.

Shawn Achor, author and happiness researcher, calls retraining our brain 'to scan for the good things in life – to help us see more possibility, to feel more energy, and to succeed at higher levels' the *positive Tetris effect.* [5] He argues that the popular game Tetris has a tendency to have such an impression on players that, after it's been shut off, people still see Tetris blocks in real life. According to Achor, 'The good news is that we can also train our brains to scan for the positive – for the possibilities dormant in every situation – and become experts at capitalising on the Happiness Advantage.'[6]

What do you believe?

Listed below are some of the good qualities, virtues or values that we like to see in people. Study it and add your own if they are not there.[7]

Ambition	Assertiveness	Beauty
Courage	Creativity	Compassion
Cooperation	Determination	Diligence
Effort	Empathy	Enthusiasm
Energy	Faith	Fitness
Flexibility	Forgiveness	Generosity
Gratitude	Health	Honesty
Honour	Humility	Idealism
Independence	Kindness	Love

5   Achor, *The Happiness Advantage*, p. 94.
6   Achor, *The Happiness Advantage*, p. 91.
7   See http://liveboldandbloom.com/05/values/list-of-values for a full list.

Loyalty	Modesty	Patience
Perseverance	Respect	Responsibility
Self-discipline	Tolerance	Trust
Truthfulness	Understanding	Wisdom

Figure 3.3: The values shield.

Now comes a really difficult task. Choose the most important four qualities to you – the ones which you firmly believe are the driving forces behind everything you think and do. Take those four choices and add them to your own drawing of the shield (Figure 3.3).

Now imagine that you can use this shield in your life to protect you against becoming a slave to impulsive actions that create undesired outcomes. This might seem like a big claim to make, but the values you firmly believe in really can be used to protect you from succumbing to courses of action you don't agree with, or from feeling bullied by others. They can act as reference points for you when times get challenging.

Let's say your chosen core values are courage, creativity, health and honesty, but you are in a job that is making you unhappy, despite earning lots of money and having high status. Reflect upon what exactly these values mean to you, and how much your job aligns with them. Tap into your creativity to come up with a work–life plan that would preserve your health and then use your courage and honesty to tell your boss, and others, about the changes you would like to make – and why.

Maybe your chosen values are empathy, determination, tolerance and wisdom. On reflection, you might realise that aspects of your behaviour towards family members or work colleagues don't sit well with these, so think about how, using these values, you might go about putting this right.

Self-discovery isn't easy

So far, this chapter makes this journey of self-discovery and self-management seem very simple and easy – but it isn't. It is difficult and it will go wrong. You will struggle from time to time to manage your moods and emotions, to think on purpose and react positively to events, to live by your beliefs, and to seek out and respond well to feedback in order to grow.

Remember that, whatever has happened to you in the past, you can learn from these experiences, reframe them, make meaning of them and move forward. There are lots more activities to try in Chapter 9 which may help keep you on track.

Mary's story

This is a true story about a young girl we will call Mary, who had two sisters. She lost her mother at the age of six and her father at the age of eight. One sister was placed in a home and the other moved away from the area to live with foster parents. By the time Mary was ten she had lived with fifteen families – and settled with none. Eventually, as a last resort, a relative agreed to take her in. There, however, Mary was made to feel as if she was an inconvenience, a burden, by the family with whom she found herself. She was not even acknowledged by the first name given to her by her parents.

She was unloved, neglected and treated badly. No one knew about it. Mary never told anyone, and her relatives ensured it was all hushed up.

One day when she was attending her junior school, she received a certificate from the headmaster. It was for 'High Endeavour'. She was pleased, surprised and perplexed. Why her? What had she done? Why now? And anyway, she didn't understand what 'endeavour' meant. She found a dictionary and looked up the meaning. This is what it said:

'A conscientious or concerted effort towards an end; an earnest attempt.'

This was one of the few positive memorable moments of Mary's young life. An adult had seen her as a capable girl; someone who had something. She kept that warm feeling inside for years, and always tried hard to please at school.

At the age of fifteen, just when she was about to take her first exams, Mary was taken away from the family she had been with, because the authorities had finally that identified that she was being neglected. She was moved to live with another foster family.

She was married at eighteen. She had two children, but the marriage was unhappy and destructive. After her divorce, at the age of 33, Mary made the brave decision to go to college to take an A level. This was to be the turning point in her life.

She was encouraged to take a higher qualification, and after two years achieved a distinction. Mary's love of learning had been rekindled, and she was given the opportunity to take an arts degree. After three more years of study, while managing a home and caring for her two children, she came away from university with a first-class honours degree and a new man in her life, who later became her second husband.

After such a traumatic childhood, Mary had every excuse to be unhappy and feel like a victim of injustice and circumstance. But she chose not to. She chose to take control, have empathy for others, work hard, and see the world as a positive place – a place in which she finally achieved beyond her wildest dreams. She has kept this attitude ever since.

She is now a successful head teacher, author, trainer and inspiring speaker.

Her favourite story is a metaphor for her life. It is about a mule that fell down a dry well. When the local farmers heard its desperate cries and saw it in the well, they felt sorry for it but couldn't find a way to get it out. So they decided to cover it with earth and bury it quickly, to put it out of its misery.

As they shovelled earth onto the mule's back, he cried with pain and sorrow as he faced death by suffocation. Then he thought of a way to save himself. 'Shake the soil off my back, then step up on top of it and compress it,' he said. He repeated, 'Shake it off and step up' again and again. Soon the farmers saw what was happening and continued to shovel earth down the well.

As the soil continued to pour on his back, the mule steadfastly shook and stepped and shook and stepped. It was hard work, and dirty and painful, but each time he shook and stepped he travelled a little further up the well. Bit by bit he edged upwards until his dirty back was at the top and he could clamber out of the well to freedom. He looked around at the astonished faces of the farmers, shook the last of the dirt from his back, and strolled off proudly into the sunshine, ready for his next job.[8]

Maybe adversity gives us a sense of self – maybe we just see it as changes that we have not yet adapted to. Adversity doesn't mean we can't be successful and do almost anything we set our minds to when we shake it off, step up, persevere and we do not give up or make excuses.

Mary's own words

I sent my soul through the invisible
Some letter of the After-life to spell:
And by and by my Soul return'd to me
And answered 'I Myself am Heav'n and Hell.'

Verse LXVI from the Rubáiyát of Omar Khayyám

We are what we think we are.

---

8   Thanks to 'Mary' for this story.

How resilient are you?

Mary developed a resilience we should all envy. The ability to survive adversity and thrive despite all the adverse events in her life requires a certain mindset. How resilient are you? Visit http://resiliencyquiz. com/index.shtml and take the resiliency quiz to find out.

So far in this chapter you have explored who you think you are. Read on to find out how you can change who you are by changing how you think, to grow and fulfil your potential.

Reflect and review

- Use your mood monitor to understand your normal default setting and what makes you happy.
- Try taking control of your default setting. Smile more often and do things that make you happy.
- Recognise when you overreact to situations and pause, reflect, reframe.
- Get feedback about how you come across and the way you communicate.
- Notice when life is giving you feedback about what you need.
- Check out your beliefs and values so that you can ensure your values are congruent with your everyday life. If you have to compromise the things you believe in by pretending to be something you are not, it will eventually make you very unhappy.
- Reframe events in your mind by seeing a difficult situation in a different way so that you develop your resilience.
- Forgive yourself if you can't live up to your ideal every day – it is a work in progress which will take a lifetime.

Points of view

Q I am the most positive person you could meet, and I make such an effort to be upbeat despite the fact that my life is full of problems. My job is immensely stressful, as I work with the public in a health centre, where people are often rude and demanding. It's very hard to keep my temper when they fail to appreciate how lucky they are to have the NHS. My two lovely children are grown up but have money problems so I am constantly having to bail them out. My husband drives me mad with his untidiness and regular visits to the pub. So the fact that I am a cheerful soul is a remarkable achievement, but the other day someone told me that I am quite a negative person. I was shocked and very hurt by this. It's so unfair – there are so many vile and horrid people in the world, and I try hard to be the opposite! Any advice?

A Isn't it strange how a random comment can really make us question the way the world sees us? There is quite a lot of contradiction in your letter, though, which makes me think that all your challenges may leak out into your communication without you realising it. You say you are upbeat, but if you look at the words you use – 'problems', 'rude', 'demanding', 'mad', 'untidiness', 'vile', 'horrid', 'shocked', 'hurt' – there are many negative words there, which may reflect your state of mind. Perhaps you are unhappier than you think and need to make some changes. Are you putting on a front of cheeriness which may work against your long-term wellbeing? Try the self-awareness quizzes and mood monitor exercise in this book to get a real insight into how you are feeling. Then maybe you could set some goals for change. Perhaps you could change your job or set some new 'rules' for your family. You deserve some genuine happiness, which will allow your natural cheeriness to shine through.

Chapter 4

The fragile powerhouse

Understanding the paradox that is your brain

> 'Our minds influence the key activity of the brain, which then influences everything; perception, cognition, thoughts and feelings, personal relationships; they're all a projection of you.'
>
> Deepak Chopra[1]

'Your brain is the hardware of your soul' says Daniel G. Amen MD in the introduction to *Change your Brain, Change your Life*.[2] He describes research which shows you can change the actual physiology of your brain to make it work well for your success and happiness. This links to Chapter 2 when we looked at creating new neural pathways when we learn new things. It makes sense that if we can change our thinking habits we can change how we act and feel. Carol Dweck also suggests that the first step towards changing your mindset is to understand your brain and how it works.

The brain itself is a fragile, delicate structure, yet at the same time it is immensely powerful. No one knows for sure what this organ is truly capable of – yet, hence the oxymoron in the title of this chapter.

----

1   http://www.forbes.com/sites/work-in-progress/2012/12/20/deepak-chopra-on-your-super-brain-work-stress-and-creativity/#2715e4857a0b2eba26f0297d.

2   D.G. Amen MD, *Change Your Brain, Change Your Life* (New York: Three Rivers Press, 1998), p. 3.

At least 95% of what we know about the brain has been learned in the past twenty years but, throughout history, philosophers and scientists have been speculating about how our brains work. They have used metaphors to describe this, with the brain being compared to a repository for the soul, a telephone exchange, a computer, a computer network, and so on. Every day, from the moment we are born, our brains are growing, and in the process creating our sense of identity and our model of the world around us. Even though the number of neurones the brain has decreases slightly as we age, the number of connections between synapses continues to grow, especially when we do new and difficult things, which creates more neural connections.

More recently, brain scanning has revealed some of the inner workings of the brain and how different parts of it react to different stimuli. Sophisticated brain imaging is now giving us astounding insights into its workings, but even these are just pointers towards finding a real understanding of how our brains work.

This chapter looks at some of the latest research, and uses anecdotal experience, to help explain how learning can build your brain power and how anxiety can disempower you. It also aims to help you understand how to take control of your emotional responses when you know more about what causes them. Knowledge is power, but beware, some of these theories have been disputed, however, they are still useful metaphors.

Ride the tiger!

In *Mindfield* the science reporter, biologist and ex-neuroscientist Lone Frank reviewed the development of brain science around the world and recounted her experience of mood-altering drugs.[3] As a long-term

---

3   L. Frank, *Mindfield* (Oxford: Oneworld Publications, 2007).

sufferer of depression, she endured the numbing effects of the widely used SSRI (selective serotonin reuptake inhibitor) antidepressants. The chemicals did their job, and calmed her self-hatred, which originated in unhappy life events. But the emotional rollercoaster she was on descended into a 'complete abandonment to hopelessness' that paralysed her. Following this experience, Frank wanted to learn how to control her own mind when she recognised the symptoms that meant she was about to spiral into depression.

She set up what she called a cognitive 'brake system' with which she recognised that all her feelings and moods were 'just chemistry'. For her, pain, jealousy, anger and hopelessness became no more than patterns of activity in the brain. She says that accepting this was, for her, the key to understanding the power of metacognition, which I call thinking on purpose:

It allows you to step back and observe yourself with a cool and analytical pair of eyes. It's like standing in a circus ring with a roaring tiger and suddenly discovering the animal obeys commands with a light swish of the whip. With a little ingenuity, you can even hop on and ride the tiger.

Lone Frank[4]

If we accept that happiness revolves around the chemical state of our brains then, as Lone Frank suggests, this may call into question the common impression that happiness depends on being thin, rich, powerful, beautiful, having a designer kitchen or a Harley-Davidson. In today's consumer society, the media insists that satisfying our desire for material things is the key to lasting happiness. In truth, we know,

4   Frank, *Mindfield*, p. 143.

and many studies have shown, that acquiring these things has no lasting effects; they only induce a quick fix of happiness chemicals. How many people do you know who are addicted to shopping?

Having a basic understanding of how our brains work offers us the best chance of mastering that complex organ between our ears and using it to achieve a lasting happiness. If you can have an insight into the working of your brain, anxious thoughts and emotional responses become more visible and therefore manageable. With practice you can enjoy taming and training the tiger!

How clever are you, anyway?

Are you clever? In what ways are you clever? How do you know? Do you know what your IQ is? Do you measure your intelligence by what exams you passed in school?

What matters is knowing that your intelligence is not fixed. If you think you are very clever, or stupid, don't think that it has to stay that way for life. Research now shows your brain responds to use in the same way a muscle does – the more you use it, the stronger it grows, and if you don't use it, or if you abuse it, you lose it! When you learn new things, the number of connections in the brain multiplies as you grow new neural networks and strengthen existing neural pathways. The more you learn new things, the more pathways your brain cells make, so what you may have once found very hard or even impossible, such as speaking a foreign language or playing the piano, becomes easier.

Do you find you do or learn some things more easily than others? We are all clever, in one way or another. You can be clever socially, emotionally or academically, artistically, musically, mathematically, linguistically, athletically or in some other way. Psychologists have investigated intelligence and found not only that intelligence isn't fixed but also that people are naturally clever in different ways. For example, Howard Gardner identified seven distinct intelligences which everyone has to a greater or lesser degree.[5] See which of these most apply to you:

- **Bodily–kinaesthetic.** These people have a keen sense of body awareness and can use their body with precision, as dancers or surgeons do. They like touching, making things, physical activity, hands-on learning, acting or role playing, love movement, and communicate well through body language.
- **Interpersonal.** These people are really good at understanding and interacting with others. They have great empathy for others and so tend to have lots of friends. They like group activities, seminars and conversation. They love communicating with others when they are working.
- **Intrapersonal.** Inward-looking people who understand their own goals because they are in tune with their inner feelings and so, as a result, can have strong will, confidence and opinions. They are independent and tend to shy away from others. They tend to love reading, creative activities, enjoy writing diaries and privacy.
- **Verbal–linguistic.** These people are highly effective at using words and are great listeners too. They tend to think in words, not pictures, and like reading, word games and writing poetry or stories.
- **Logical–mathematical.** These people are good at reasoning, calculating and thinking conceptually about abstract ideas. They are quick to see and explore patterns and relationships, and like to experiment, solve puzzles and continually question everything.
- **Musical.** These people love music and rhythm, and are very

---

5   H. Gardner, *Frames of Mind: The theory of multiple intelligences*, 2nd edn (London: Fontana Press, 1993). An important addition to the literature of cognitive psychology, being the first full-length explanation of multiple intelligences.

aware of sounds in their environment. They can study better with music on in the background. They can remember information by turning it into rhythmical lyrics.

- **Visual–spatial**. People who are strong in this area are very aware of the physical space around them and of their position in it. They like drawing, jigsaws and reading maps. They mentally model problems and love seeing models, images, charts, graphs, photos and other visual imagery.

Gardner later added naturalistic and existential intelligences. The former suggests special skills related to nature, such as working with animals and plants, and the latter the ability to connect with people in a spiritual way.

Another, simpler way of finding out how your brain prefers to work is to use the Visual, Auditory and Kinaesthetic (VAK) learning style model put forward by Fleming (2001).[6] According to this, most people have a dominant or preferred learning style and others have a blend of the three styles:

- **Visual learners** learn through seeing and think in pictures, creating visual metaphors and analogies. They need to create strong mental images to remember information, and enjoy looking at maps, charts, pictures, videos, and movies. Their visual skills help them to have a good sense of direction and to see patterns in charts and graphs. They like fixing things.
- **Auditory learners** tend to learn through listening. They are very good listeners and are generally good at speaking and presenting, writing, storytelling, explaining, teaching, using humour and arguing their point of view. They think in words rather than

---

6   N.D. Fleming, *Teaching and Learning Styles: VARK strategies* (published by the author, Christchurch, New Zealand, 5th edition, 2001).

pictures, and learn best through lectures, discussions, talking things through, and listening to what others have to say.

■ **Kinaesthetic learners** tend to learn through moving, doing and touching. They have a good sense of balance and hand–eye coordination, and find it hard to sit still for long periods. They may become distracted by their need for activity and exploration. They remember and process information through interacting with the space around them. They have good athletic ability, like hands-on experimentation, using body language, crafts, acting, miming, using their hands to create or build, dancing, and expressing emotions using their body.

The VAK model has been widely disputed in recent years, as many people were tempted to pigeonhole others as V, A or K learners and then encourage activities that only suited this learning style. For example, kinaesthetic learners who enjoyed sport were encouraged to spend more time doing physical activity, whereas they actually needed to practise auditory and visual skills as well, so that they could develop a more flexible learning style. It is particularly important for children to have a wide range of challenges that help them develop V, A and K skills, rather than just doing what they are 'good' at. If learners work harder on the styles they find most difficult they will develop more resilience when life offers challenges later. It's good to know our strengths and preferences as learners so we can become expert in certain fields, but a flexible approach that is willing to challenge our own learning comfort zones will be a great asset in future employment. This is the essence of a growth mindset. If you find maths hard – do more of it!

It is best to keep a healthy scepticism about any theories about learning – there is no one-size-fits-all model. Find out what works best for you as you try growing your potential and performance, and always try to add to your repertoire of learning strategies.

One of the most important discoveries psychologists have made regards the extent to which we are able to grow our own brains as a result of our life experiences. This ability to grow – due the 'plasticity' of the brain – has provided a huge breakthrough in our understanding of how to live a happier and more successful life. Growing our brains by learning and relearning is both possible and desirable. It is possible because we now know we can improve our skills and wisdom at any time of life. It is desirable because when we achieve something, after having to work and think hard, the satisfaction we get is happiness inducing! In addition, it's empowering to know that, although the brain has the greatest potential to make new connections when we are young, it continues for the rest of our lives. One of the secrets to fighting off dementia is to keep learning. It also means that, regardless of what you achieved at school, your learning journey can begin again at any time.

In his book *The Power of Habit*, Charles Duhigg examines the neuroscience of how habits form and makes it clear that it is really important to look at, and acknowledge, and, when needed, challenge our default settings. When we are acting through habit we aren't choosing but instead are behaving automatically, without thinking. Of habits he said: 'Then we stopped making a choice and the behaviour became automatic. It's a natural consequence of our neurology. And by understanding how it happens, you can rebuild those patterns in whichever way you choose.'[7]

Many of us also need to realise that much of our behaviour is not a choice because it has been programmed into our unconscious and has become a habit. A good example of this is habits that have become obsessive. Compulsively washing your hands, checking the door is locked, stepping over pavement cracks and so on can come to dominate some people's thinking so that these behaviours are no longer a

---

7   C. Duhigg, *The Power of Habit* (London: Random House, 2012), p. xvii.

choice but a habitual way of relieving anxiety. These patterns need to be dismantled and rebuilt. Having the cognitive flexibility to understand such behaviours is the first step towards freedom from the tyranny of obsessive thinking.

Andrew Curran studied research into the human brain and came to the simple, but telling, conclusion that our: 'unique human ability [is] to be able to turn our thoughts inwards and observe ourselves and our own mental life. This is an extraordinarily powerful observation because it is only through this ability that you can understand your own emotions and hence the emotions of others'.[8] This ability to think on purpose and reflect on how we react in various situations, rather than think instinctively, requires what Daniel Goleman called emotional intelligence. This is a measure of our ability to 'rein in emotional impulse; to read another's innermost feelings; to handle relationships smoothly'.[9] Or, as Aristotle put it, 'to be angry with the right person, to the right degree at the right time, for the right purpose and in the right way'.[10]

When we think on purpose, we should use our emotional intelligence to think in a way that will take us towards our goal of making ourselves, and others, happy. The EQ required to take control of your thoughts and feelings is much more important than any notion of IQ, fixed or not. So if we have developed EQ and a modicum of IQ, why are we still so prone to irrational, instinctive behaviour?

8   A. Curran, The Little Book of Big Stuff About the Brain (Carmarthen: Crown House Publishing, 2008), p. 22.
9   D. Goleman, Emotional Intelligence: Why it can matter more than IQ (London: Bloomsbury, 1996), p. xiii.
10   Quoted in Edith M. Leonard, Lillian E. Miles and Catherine S. Van der Kar, The Child: At home and school (New York: American Book Company, 1944), p. 203.

The three-part brain

P.D. MacLean's simple description of the triune (three-part) brain immediately helps us to understand a little more about why we can get hijacked by our emotions.[11] He said that we can divide the brain into three regions: the reptilian brain, the limbic brain and the neocortex.

The reptilian brain controls our survival and territorial instincts which kick in when we feel threatened; the limbic system deals with our emotional engagement and interpersonal nurturing behaviours; and the neocortex is involved with higher-order thinking skills. This is shown in Figure 4.1.

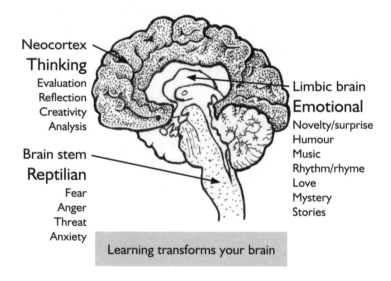

Figure 4.1: The three-part brain.

---

11   P.D. MacLean, *A Triune Concept of the Brain and Behavior* (Toronto: University of Toronto Press, 1973).

But before we get into detail about how the triune brain affects our behaviour, let's look at some astonishing facts about the brain. According to Andrew Curran in his book *The Little Book of Big Stuff About the Brain*, our reptilian brain has only 15–20 million neurones, the emotional brain (or limbic system) has about 100 million neurones, but there are up to 100 billion (100,000 million) neurones in a fully developed brain. If these were laid end to end they would stretch for 100,000 miles![12]

Each neurone can be connected to 1,000–10,000 other neurones via little bridges called synapses. This means there may be between 100 trillion and 1,000 trillion (1,000 million million) synaptic connections. Because no one is sure how memories are laid down in the brain, estimates of its memory capacity vary enormously from 1 to 1,000 terabytes. (For comparison, the 19 million volumes in the US Library of Congress represent about 10 terabytes of data.[13] These mind-boggling numbers give just a flavour of the astounding complexity of our brains, and their untapped potential. Phew! Let's go back to the simple three-part brain …

The reptile inside your head

The reptilian brain is the oldest, most primitive part of our brains. It keeps your heart beating, your food travelling through your gut and your blood pumping around your body, but it has one overriding function and that is to 'preserve its own existence'.[14] For 400 million years it has helped mammals survive the dangers that surround them. And it is still doing its job of protecting you by reacting to pain and any

---

12 See http://discovermagazine.com/2011/mar/10-numbers-the-nervous-system.
13 See http://www.human-memory.net/brain_neurons.html.
14 A. Curran, *The Little Book of Big Stuff About the Brain* (Carmarthen: Crown House Publishing, 2008), p. 7.

other perceived threats to your safety. And therein lies a problem.

In the 21st century, the threats to our existence are very different to what they used to be, but our reptilian brain is still primed to kick into action in the same way. Any of your fears, phobias or anxieties will be seen by your reptilian brain as a threat. When the reptilian brain kicks in, you get an adrenalin rush, which transfers blood away from your skin. The blood is diverted instead to your muscles so that you can get ready to either fight or flee from the threat. Your heart rate and blood pressure go up to make sure that the blood flow to the muscles is further increased, and your breathing changes, to load up your blood with more oxygen.

This adrenalin-fuelled 'fight or flight' reaction helped our ancestors fight or run away very fast from threats like predators or attack by other people. It had such great survival value that it became an automatic response to perceived threats. But this reaction is not very useful to us when the perceived threat is a harmless spider or a mouse. Neither is it useful when you are standing on the edge of a cliff suffering from vertigo, sitting on an aircraft about to take off, or about to go and make a speech you have been dreading.

The reaction to these perceived threats can be just as powerful as if your existence was in danger, bringing on the adrenalin rush and all the associated physical symptoms. When this happens, especially unexpectedly, the physical symptoms can make us feel so out of control that they can induce terror and lead to panic attacks. If this happens just as you are about to make an important speech, for example, it is no wonder that the threat (the speech) and the reaction to it become so closely entwined that it leads to people doing all they can to avoid the perceived threat in future. Understand that anxiety – and its scary symptoms – is simply your brain reacting to a perceived threat; it is only trying to help you survive. Recognising and believing this may enable you to manage and control these feelings more effectively.

It may be useful to think of anxiety as lying on a spectrum of feelings (see Figure 4.2).

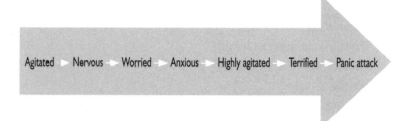

Figure 4.2: The spectrum of anxiety.

The perceived threats in our world which move you along this spectrum are far less likely to be the sight of a predator or axe-murderer, and far more likely to be a thought: a thought which our mind associates with feeling threatened. This can be anything from learning to drive, through to going to a party alone, dating, flying abroad or taking an exam: anything that your brain perceives as unfamiliar, unusual, unknown or unresolved is to some degree classified as a threat. In other words, anything that could take you outside your comfort zone could induce feelings of anxiety. So, if you are learning something new or putting yourself in an unfamiliar situation, especially if you don't do this very often, your reptilian brain could bring on some nasty fearful feelings.

Anxiety is a wave that can wash over you, if you let it.
See it this way: FEAR = Feel Everything And Recover

Would any of the following situations register on the above spectrum for you? Copy down the anxiety spectrum in Figure 4.2 and place some of these situations on the spectrum, to help you understand what is outside your comfort zone. (For more practical exercises like this, see Chapter 9.)

Parachuting
Travelling alone on an aircraft
Standing on the edge of a cliff
Driving at night
Walking alone into a party
Catching a Tube train in London
Meeting a large loose dog
Eating shellfish
Singing a karaoke song (sober!)
Asking a neighbour to move their car
Breaking down on the motorway
Attending a personal training session
Cooking for a dinner party
Giving emergency first aid if someone collapses in front of you

Challenge yourself to try one of the things that make you feel anxious. Make it easier by enlisting the help of friends to complete the challenge.

There is also another problem here. Later on, when the thinking brain gets in on the act, it can start thinking up some sort of 'rational' justification for these feelings. It does this by creating an inner dialogue that 'explains' your reaction. This can be a real problem because the thinking part of the brain is very clever at making connections with previous experiences and at producing limiting beliefs that seem to make sense, like 'I'm no good at this' or 'If I try doing … it always goes wrong and I'll show myself up.' This means that when a situation which we see as a threat comes to mind, the thinking brain immediately conjures up the limiting belief and the fears associated with it.

The reptilian brain promptly seizes on this and this sets off the series of physical responses.

The last time I felt like this, I was in front of an interview panel. I had prepared well for the interview, but my head was full of negative inner dialogue that provoked debilitating physical symptoms. I felt afraid and my heart was beating so hard that I couldn't think, let alone talk. Time seemed to stand still. I was inside my own head thinking that these people were judging me and would find me lacking. My brain detected a threat and was preparing my body to run away. Of course, these feelings of panic and fear undermined my performance. I didn't get the job.

Once you recognise that this is happening, it is time to step back and think on purpose – to work out *why* you are feeling tense and anxious. If you learn to do this, you can reassure your thinking brain that the situation is not a threat, that you (or others), are not to blame, and cut out the reptilian brain response. If, after thinking on purpose, you are still puzzled by your inexplicable mood swings or irrational feelings, then a good therapist may be able to help.

Anxiety is just your brain trying to protect you from perceived danger.

Joe would find himself standing outside the door at parties, sweating and hesitating to go in, even though he really wanted to. Why did he feel like this? As he was approaching the door his thinking brain would remember times when he couldn't join in the social chit-chat, which he told himself he wasn't good at. Worse, he remembered the times he found himself standing alone in a corner because no one would speak to him, and he felt that others were judging him. These conscious fears triggered the reptilian brain to produce physical symptoms, which

magnified the problem. Often all his previous failed attempts at joining in would also come to mind, leading to a negative spiral of
thoughts. So Joe would walk away, too nervous to enter, because that
meant trying to overcome his fears and limiting beliefs.

Most of us have had similar experiences when our primitive
brain escalated a situation, heightening our anxieties and shifting
them towards uncontrollable panic where our feelings get in the way
of being able to rationalise what's happening. Avoiding interviews or
walking away from a party will only reinforce the fear. It will confirm
that, yes, this is risky and that you are right to panic about it. As a
result, the next time you are outside the door of an interview room,
or a party, the symptoms will be even stronger and harder to control.
Breaking down negative beliefs and overcoming fear is an important
part of reprogramming your thinking brain and short-circuiting
your primitive brain's reaction to the situation. Read on to find out
how to reprogramme your brain and walk through those imaginary
doors.

Thoughts change minds

Controlling the switch in our thinking brain that turns on the reptilian
brain is not only vital for overcoming our fears and limiting beliefs, it
is also vital for growing our emotional intelligence. This is because the
reptilian brain reacts to the fear and anxiety caused by limiting beliefs
and also to long-term worries. As we've seen, it does this by, among
other things, causing the release of adrenalin. If we experience a dra-
matic event or trauma, a large amount of adrenalin is released.

If this happens in a school, social or work situation, we can't literally run away from the cause or punch the living daylights out of it.
(Well, we could – but with what consequences?) So what happens to
all the excess energy that the adrenalin surge causes? It gets channelled

into physical symptoms like raised blood pressure and increased heart rate, or into triggering emotions like anger, rage and anxiety. Long-term worries cause a long-term, low-level release of adrenalin and other anxiety-related hormones. The effect of this is a feeling of increased mental pressure which, along with a range of associated physical and mental symptoms, leads to the condition we call stress.

The physical symptoms of stress (such as sweating, blushing and shaking) are unpleasant enough, but long-term effects can include high blood pressure, heart disease, muscle tension, ulcers, irritable bowel, headaches and a reduced immune response. Mental symptoms can include outbursts of anger, long-term irritability and sleeplessness, lack of concentration, anxiety, and low self-esteem. These feelings can feed on each other and end up causing depression.

When thinking is just as scary

We can also experience anxiety when there is no real threat and just the thought of something scares us.

How can this happen? Our memory and imagination are very closely linked in our thinking brains, so that when we think of a situation we have been in, we can instantly remember our feelings at the time. If these are not good memories, then our reptilian brain reacts as if the situation is really happening, and causes the physical symptoms of anxiety.

For example, if someone suggests going pot-holing and you have a fear of enclosed spaces, your stomach can literally turn as you imagine the experience. In my case, there was a time when if someone just suggested I could give a talk in a meeting the next week, my knees would turn to jelly. I would then go on to compound the reaction by mentally rehearsing the disaster that awaited me, thinking about how

I would dry up, go into panic mode and have to leave the room.

Catastrophic thinking like this reinforces our thinking brain's perception that the situations we fear pose a real danger. To compound this, the reptilian brain will then automatically – and unconsciously – react with an even stronger response, which amplifies our conscious fear, and so on, leading to a vicious circle. It is no wonder that we can become quivering wrecks, incapable of calling upon our resilience and other resources when we actually have to tackle the pot hole or make that speech.

This also explains why recalling a terrible event in a court room (of being mugged or raped, for example) can feel like being abused all over again. In this situation the brain doesn't seem to differentiate between real and imagined terror. The mere memory of the event creates the same emotional response which triggers the reptilian brain, leading to physical symptoms.

Controlling the reptile

Our brains are continuously making sense of our daily life, seeking patterns and connections with past experience in order to assess whether anything in our environment is a threat to our survival. For example, you enter an interview room and your brain checks its memories. It recognises the atmosphere, the seating pattern, the panel of interviewers and creates a reaction, based on its memory of previous interview situations. If the past memories are bad or the interview begins to go badly, the reaction may not be useful. Your voice becomes shaky, your heart beats faster, your mind goes blank – just when you need to be at your very best.

It feels as though your brain is letting you down. You become more conscious of how you look and feel, you become emotional. You find yourself getting distracted, less able to concentrate and get the feeling that it is all slipping away from you. No wonder people are tempted to self-medicate with alcohol or other drugs to inhibit those unwanted responses. The trouble is, they can also blunt your thinking.

It takes mind control to master your nerves and be at your best in these situations. You need to think on purpose before and during the event, so that you act as if you are calm, controlled and powerful. If you can train yourself how to do this every time you have a similar experience, this approach will start to become second nature.

First, you should search your memory for the last time you had an interview, exam or hot date – whatever is making you feel anxious. Then, rehearse the things that went well and examine the things that did not. Don't think catastrophically about the bad things; look at them dispassionately, coolly and calmly. Dissect what went wrong and think of strategies to avoid this happening next time. Rehearse these strategies, all the time checking how they are working. See yourself using them and growing in confidence and fluency. Think about how you know this situation is an opportunity, rather than a threat, and how it will energise you instead of paralysing you. One way to do this is to have mantras in place that highlight the best beliefs and breathing techniques, which replicate the calm, controlled body sensations you want to experience. It will work if you believe it will and it will work so long as you put in the practice beforehand (see some visualisation examples on p. 178).

So what else can we do to tame our brain and manage our nerves? Try this next time you are going to do something that you find challenging and which you know would normally bring on feelings of fear or nervousness:

Remind yourself that you now understand that anxiety is only your brain's way of protecting you from perceived danger. Reassure your brain that this situation is not actually life-threatening and, if the symptoms of anxiety have already been triggered, deliberately manage them. The following strategies might be helpful:

- Breathe slowly and deliberately, enhancing feelings of calm and wellbeing.
- Provide an alternative focus, such as counting slowly in twos to 100.
- Exercise. Stretching or walking is good.
- Use a mantra that has a message of strength, e.g. 'I am calm, cool and powerful'.
- Reframe limiting beliefs such as 'I just can't do it' to 'I can and will do it.'
- Visualise yourself doing the scary thing and it going very well. This takes effort and practice.

The most successful performers are not completely without nerves – they are simply the ones who have learned to handle their nerves on the big day. They visualise success and can channel their nervous energy into delivering a great performance.

Dr Steve Peters has trained some of the world's top sports performers. In *The Chimp Paradox*[15] he created a really useful metaphor, an ill-behaved chimp, to help us manage our thinking and our emotions. His model is based on tested scientific principles, and helps you remove anxiety and develop emotional skills. It does this by getting you to see parts of your brain, and your responses to events, as your own personal mischievous chimp, who needs to be kept under control. He gives useful advice and exercises on how to do this, such as 'boxing' your chimp and feeding it bananas! This is another way of explaining how to manage and control your thoughts. His work with famous sporting stars, such as cyclist Victoria Pendleton and snooker player Ronnie O'Sullivan, using this model, has enabled them and

15 S. Peters, *The Chimp Paradox* (London: Random House, 2012).

many others to overcome their personal demons and achieve the highest accolades in their field.

There are many ways to control your reptilian brain once you know why it kicks in. The 'fight or flight' response has ensured our survival as a species. Knowing that you can take control of it will help you tap into the powerhouse that is your brain, so that you will grow.

Every time your brain tells you to be afraid, step back and think on purpose. Ask yourself, 'Is this really a threat to my survival?' 'Is this really as bad as I imagine it is?' 'Am I taking this too seriously?' Trust that you will survive, that you will know what to do, that you can act as if you're not afraid. And then persevere!

Learn from each occasion in which you try to overcome your fears. What worked well? What could you do even better? Always respond positively to any feedback and bounce back, ready to give it another go. Don't try to eat the whole elephant in one bite. If possible, cut the problem into bite-sized chunks and deal with them one at a time. Try it! Do the things that scare you most first. If you do, you will grow in confidence and become less fearful. It doesn't matter whether the strategy you tried worked first time or not, because you're still alive to try again!

Consider: in which situations do I need to push myself through the fear barrier and do it anyway?

How did I overcome my fear of public speaking?

First, I had to be honest with myself. I had to admit my fear and the fact that it was becoming debilitating to myself. I then went on to recognise that my fear was irrational – after all, public speaking is not in itself a dangerous activity – but that, even so, it affected me in certain situations. This helped me to see the problem more clearly and to get it into proportion. I began to feel less ashamed and secretive about it and started admitting to close friends that I was terrified of speaking in public.

Often their response would be astonishment: 'But you seem so super-confident – I don't believe it!' Other friends would tell me they felt the same, which made me realise that I was not alone. Strangely, I felt that these fellow sufferers would also sympathise with me in the struggles which I knew lay ahead, now that I felt strong enough to challenge my fear. Then I began my plan to desensitise my brain.

I consciously got out of my comfort zone and volunteered to help a local young mothers' group. I made sure I took on a role which would involve having to do a tiny bit of speaking, but which I could control. I avoided being secretary because reading out the minutes would floor me! After a little while I could introduce visitors and contribute to, and even help run, a few meetings. This boosted my confidence enough to join a local public speaking group. Here I met many people who had all sorts of reasons to be terrified. They ranged from people with stammers and lisps to people like barristers, aspiring shop managers, and sales reps who had to deliver talks or reports or lead and motivate teams – or face losing their jobs.

Every week I saw people who were much more afraid than I was, and this was a humbling experience. I would watch the others at my group speak in a quavering voice, sometimes with their whole body shaking. The empathy I felt often made watching this almost as bad as delivering the speech myself! My stomach would tie itself up in knots and I would live their pain. But seeing them be so brave helped make me even more determined to beat my demons and find a way to break through the fear.

We would all practise delivering speeches to our group using prompt cards, and would be evaluated on our performance. Although this was my idea of hell, I learned a lot about how to speak formally. Every week I reminded myself that I had a massively supportive audience who wanted to give me kind, specific and helpful feedback. I also managed to overcome the initial dread by mentally rehearsing everything going well before the event and learning to focus outwards on the message and the audience instead of inwards on myself. This helped quieten my panicky thoughts and gradually stopped me getting distracted by them. After each speech I felt elated because I had survived, but inside, I still felt that I could never deliver a speech to anyone else outside the safe confines of my group.

Afterwards, in the pub I would challenge myself to speak to, and in front of, others just a little more each time. At community meetings and meetings at work I would ask questions – even though my heart felt that it would beat its way out of my chest. As I was doing this, I developed some useful mantras for challenging my belief that I would never be able to speak in public comfortably. This is what I told myself: 'I love public speaking and it is what I was born for!' I was starting to act 'as if', and this thought helped me reframe my negative mindset every time the panic bubbled up inside.

Then one day at my speaking group we upped the ante with an interesting activity – we videoed each other's speeches. I gave a five-minute talk on a recent disastrous attempt to ski. Later, when I watched the video of me telling the story, I was truly shocked by it. I looked so cool, calm and confident. I was even vaguely amusing! I couldn't believe that I could look as if I was enjoying it in the video but feel such panic in my head and body.

This was a turning point for me because I realised that my fear was all about other people seeing me scared and uncomfortable – and feeling sorry for me. But if I didn't *look* nervous, then it didn't matter if I felt panicky inside. I could use my breathing strategies and focus on the message, knowing that as far as the audience was concerned I looked confident.

The rest of the story is not a quick fix. It took months in my public speaking group to find the strategies that worked for me, and years of accepting gradually greater and greater speaking challenges before I was able to speak fluently and confidently in front of often very large audiences. Finally, it has only been in the last few years that I have been able to tell my audiences that I used to be terrified of public speaking. This often causes astonishment, because I now present with energy, confidence and, people tell me, inspiration.

Now I really do love public speaking and feel I was born for it. My mantra came true! I am so glad I chose to do the thing that scared me so much – because now, nothing scares me!

The emotional brain

The other vital part of the brain we need to understand if we want to grow is the emotional brain, or the limbic system. This is concerned with more complex behaviours such as socialising and caring for our young, and is where our memories are made. It responds to music and is fascinated by rhyme and rhythm. This is why advertisers sell things to us using catchy slogans that we find it hard to forget – such as 'Just do it'.

Good conversationalists and speakers engage the emotional brains of their listeners, whether that is one person or many. Think of what makes an interesting speaker: they tell stories that engage our emotions, stories which have humour and mystery, and they do so using eye contact and animated body language. They also exude passion and belief, all of which taps into the emotional brain and makes what they say interesting and memorable.

However, the most powerful way to engage the emotional brain of people you speak to is by making them feel loved and valued. Whether you are socialising, selling or trying to advise family or colleagues, there is nothing more powerful than making someone else feel cared for. Whatever your age or status, when you communicate with genuine empathy and understanding, you make a connection that will produce a better outcome. This takes flexibility and good listening skills, which you can read about in Chapter 7.

Andrew Curran investigated how you can be more effective at persuading, convincing, negotiating, motivating, influencing or teaching others. His conclusion was: 'All it takes is love'.[16] If you consider the most powerful influencers in your life, they will probably be people who really seem to 'get' or understand you. They are able to empathise with you, listen to your point of view, and appreciate your finer points without seeming to flatter. They have built up a bond of trust with you. They are able to push you onwards because you genuinely believe in them and that they can help develop your potential. Feeling those positive emotions in conversation and unconsciously bonding with someone helps us engage with one another.

If giving and getting love can make such a positive difference to the outcomes of our interactions with others, why aren't we all at it? One reason may be that, in normal conversation, we don't consciously fake genuine care for others. It's either there, or it is not. If it isn't, then it's usually easy for us to sense when someone is being nice just to get our business or get their own way.

Being able to cultivate real empathy and rapport is an essential ingredient to success in business or family life. Can you do this? Or do

---

16 Curran, *The Little Book of Big Stuff About the Brain*, p. 1.

you have relatives or people at work that you want, or need, to get on with, but somehow don't? Can you learn how to form rapport? The answer is yes. Think of successful con artists. They have learned how to deliberately manipulate the emotional brains of their victims to gain their trust. You, too, can think on purpose and fake it to make it. It may sound wrong to use the conversational strategies below and fake genuine interest in others, but if the outcome is better relationships with them, it can't all be bad!

- **Listen** – really listen to the feelings and beliefs being expressed and try to understand the other person's map of the world.
- **Don't judge** – you can disagree, but still see their point of view.
- **Respect** the individual and their needs.
- **Be open** about your own thoughts and feelings – self-disclosure develops trust. (For more practical strategies for developing your communication skills, see Chapter 7.)

The thinking brain

The third part of the triune brain is the very complex neocortex. It is capable of thousands of behaviours. For example, it enables us to have a sense of past and future, recall memories, create metaphors and to tell stories. Our ability to evaluate, analyse, review, create and learn all reside here. It is the neocortex that sets us apart from other animals. It helps us make plans and think of solutions to challenges, as well as decide what to cook for dinner!

The neocortex is also where learning happens and where we can accumulate knowledge and skills. There is evidence that, the more we use our higher-order thinking and stretch our brainpower, the cleverer we become. Brain scans have shown that when London cabbies study the gruelling 'The Knowledge' qualification (for which they have to know every street in London), the part of their brain linked to memory grows bigger.[17]

It is in the neocortex that 'thinking on purpose' goes on. Metacognition gives us the unique ability to observe ourselves and reflect on how our amazing brain is working for us – and take more control of it. As a result of thinking on purpose, the neocortex is also capable of massive change. It can learn and grow new neural pathways, which can make the best of what the emotional brain can offer and, as we have seen, learn to keep the primitive brain under control.

Reflect and review

- The brain is massively powerful and plastic. It's useful to think of our brains growing and changing like a muscle as we learn.
- There are many different ways to be clever; everyone learns in their own unique way.
- Understanding the brain helps us take control of our thinking.
- The three-part brain theory helps us to understand anxiety and engagement.
- The reptilian brain can create powerful physical symptoms of fear if it feels threatened.
- Anxiety is your brain trying to protect you.
- Your emotional brain needs to be engaged to get motivated and learn.
- You are increasing the number of neural pathways in your neocortex every time you learn something new.
- You are in control of growing your own brain – or not.

---

17 See http://www.bbc.co.uk/news/health-16086233.

Points of view

Q I have a terror of balloons, which seems to be getting worse as I get older. Most of the time it doesn't matter, because I don't come across them, but at children's parties or celebrations where balloons are around, I get in such a panic I have to leave. Even the thought of a balloon makes me shake. Don't try telling me to learn to love balloons, because I tried that with spiders and it made it worse. How can you learn to love what you hate?

I have my best friend's wedding coming up, and I am so afraid that she will have helium balloons decorating the reception venue, so I will have to leave. As I'm her bridesmaid, this would be really embarrassing. Please help.

A I really understand this type of illogical terror that creates physical symptoms of panic and nausea. Your brain has detected a threat and is trying to protect you from a balloon! It sounds silly when you think of it like that, but it is worth trying to think about what exactly it is about the balloon that creates this reaction. Is it the feel, the potential bang, the colours?

If you want to change this reaction you need to reprogramme your brain. Start by visualising yourself blowing up a balloon – just for a little while. Then imagine squishing it and squashing it, perhaps even sitting on it, then letting the air out. Feel calm and relaxed as you do this again – and blow it up a little bigger each time. Yes, you are learning to love balloons and change your response. But so far you haven't actually touched one. Eventually, and preferably with a helper, you can do all this in real life.

Unfortunately, the only way to change your thinking is to change your memories of balloons until your brain doesn't see them as a threat. But wouldn't it be worth it? Once you have learned this method you can apply it to a fear of spiders too. The alternative is that you never learn to manage fear, and your anxiety spreads and latches on to other things.

Chapter 5

If you believe you can,
or believe you can't,
you're right

The mindset for learning

In Chapter 2 we explored how our fundamental beliefs and values provide a frame through which we see the world and so provide the scaffolding for the stage on which our lives are acted out.

Our beliefs and values also colour the language we use in our internal dialogue as we deal with everyday events. This, in turn, determines how we see the world and influences how we perceive success and happiness. Depending on what we believe and value, our internal dialogue can give rise to thoughts which are either limiting or empowering. As they continually pop into our heads, these thoughts have the power to help shape our future because they reinforce themselves and can become self-fulfilling prophecies for good – or ill.

For example, have you ever heard your internal voice say negative things such as:

- I'm just unlucky.
- I can never remember names.
- I'm no good at sports/maths/music/science …
- Cooking isn't my thing.

- Relationships always go wrong for me.
- I'm useless at following maps.
- I can't dance/sing/paint/draw/spell/speak in front of an audience …

Any of the statements above may first come from a half-truth based on some past evidence from our experience. We can then reinforce it by telling other people – and ourselves – the same message again and again, until it begins to predict the future. For example, if you discovered at school that you found writing hard, perhaps because you had undiagnosed dyslexic tendencies, you may have believed that you were 'stupid' compared to other children. Worse still, because of this perception, you would then probably have avoided doing the most important thing needed to improve your writing skills – which was to do more and more writing. This state of affairs could have persisted until you discovered that intelligence isn't just measured by your ability to form letters.

There are many famous people who are dyslexic, such as Richard Branson, John Lennon, George Washington, Leonardo da Vinci and Albert Einstein. They found huge success in life, despite early challenges, and achieved what they did because they had drive and determination, alongside a relentless belief in their own potential. Their early experiences of struggling with literacy didn't prevent them from fulfilling their destiny.

You might wonder if these people were simply destined to be brilliant. However, Matthew Syed suggests in his book *Bounce*[1] that there is no such thing as innate talent. He says it wasn't the myth of innate talent that took them, or any other successful person, to the top in their field. Instead, the key to their success lay in many hours of purposeful, focused practice to improve their ability to expert level. In

---

1   M. Syed, *Bounce* (London: Fourth Estate, 2011).

Outliers,[2] Malcolm Gladwell claims that it takes about 10,000 hours of practice for people to become an expert. (If the 10,000 hours were completed as eight-hour days, five days a week, with no other holidays, you would be practising like this for five years to achieve excellence!) However, this claim is something of an oversimplification because it omits three of the most essential elements for continued improvement. First, that you must begin by directing your efforts towards the things you find hardest to do or which someone (with knowledge) has pointed out that you need to do. Second, that you also need to give the practice your full and continued attention. (Even if doing something starts to become second nature, you have to keep working on it to improve it further.)

Third, you also need to get feedback – and, crucially, act on it. As Daniel Goleman says of the 10,000-hour rule in *Focus*: 'The problem: it's only half true. If you are a duffer at golf, say, and make the same mistakes every time you try a certain swing or putt, 10,000 hours of practising that error will not improve your game. You'll still be a duffer, albeit an older one.'[3]

The main predictor of success is *deliberate* practice – persistent training to which you give your full concentration, rather than just your time, and where you are guided by a skilled expert, coach, or mentor. Pay attention to what you are practising: quality practice is not just about putting in the hours. To do this you need to think on purpose – concentrate on learning, be curious about how to improve your skills and knowledge through research and getting feedback – and put any limiting beliefs to one side. There will be many trials on the way, but be persistent and remember that we all learn through setbacks.

For example, if cooking isn't your thing, then do more of it. Learn from experts and improve your skills by practising lots of different

---

2   M. Gladwell, *Outliers: The story of success* (London: Penguin, 2008), pp. 39–42.
3   D. Goleman, *Focus: The hidden driver of excellence* (London: Bloomsbury, 2014), p. 163.

recipes. If you struggle with computers, then get advice when you are stuck – either from an expert who will show you what to do, or online from someone else who has cracked the problem – and practise that particular skill immediately. The more you look for and use what you learn, the more proficient you will become.

There is always the temptation to simply get someone else to do it for you. But if you do this, you lose your chance to learn and develop new skills. If you can't use a map and get lost easily it's tempting, for example, to invest in a satnav, but this will mean you will never develop your map-reading skills.

Mark's story

Mark's sense of direction was never good. He instinctively tended to go the wrong way, whether in a car or even coming out of his hotel room on his way to reception. 'I'm hopeless at directions' was the mantra he used to explain to others why he always seemed to get lost. But buying a satnav changed his life. Now he had no need to struggle with maps or go to the effort of planning his route. He could now drive cross-country and through big cities and not worry about how he would reach his destination. Gleefully, he threw away all his maps.

However, once, when Mark was halfway to a place he had been to several times before, his satnav died. He looked around and realised he had no idea where he was or how to get to his destination – or how to return home. With no road map in the car, he was stuck. He had been spoon-fed instructions for this journey instead of working out the route on a map and remembering landmarks and signposts. After all, you don't need to do that if you have a satnav! Unfortunately, when his satnav died he found out that he had disabled his spatial awareness still further.

His reaction was to become even more convinced that he was useless at directions. He quickly bought another satnav, and avoided tackling his underlying self-belief.

Consequently, even today if he is on a group outing, Mark is still in the habit of saying, 'I'm useless at directions. You take the lead.' He is still feeding his limiting belief and confirming its truth.

This is in contrast to Mark's friend John, who enjoys his ability to use the satnav in his head and who continually challenges himself to find his own way by a mixture of instinct and signposts. John gets better and better at finding his way round because he is constantly challenging his brain to make new connections and further develop his mental mapping ability. Meanwhile, Mark gets less confident and less effective because he avoids using the very part of his brain that needs the extra practice. 'At least someone knows where we're going,' he thinks, as he sits in the back of the car or hovers on the sidelines on a group hike through the hills.

We should treat negative or limiting beliefs as challenges to our belief systems. Change 'I'm not good at directions' to a belief that 'I'm not good at directions … *yet.*' Then identify exactly what you are going to do to work on your spatial skills (and who you might ask for tips on how to do it). Seek out someone like John. Learn what signs and landmarks to look out for, and how to use a map to plan your route.

Note down the road numbers and directions and mentally rehearse travelling the route. You could use Street View to see what various places along the journey look like, so that they become landmarks that you can recognise so that you know you're on the right track. Try travelling the route using only your notes, with a satnav as a back-up. On the journey, try to make mental, or (when you're not driving) even written, notes of memorable landmarks, signposts, road names, shops, and so on. Challenge yourself to remember the way the second time. Switch off the satnav and only use your notes. If you have passengers in the car, give them a running commentary, telling them how you are navigating the route. Repeat this until you can do the journey unaided. Copy this strategy for other journeys until you have built up your skills and moved beyond that limiting belief.

Every time you hear yourself express a limiting belief, add the word 'yet' to open up the possibility of change.

One of the problems with tackling our habitual limiting beliefs is that we don't really want others to see us become baby learners again. If someone else was in the car with Mark and saw his list of directions, landmarks and so on, then Mark might feel embarrassed to be seen needing such aids – especially as men think they are the masters of navigation! But to create new neural pathways, all learning needs to go back to basics. Reframe the experience. Admit that you have a problem, and tell yourself you have resolved to do something about it. Don't forget to praise yourself for progress and if you can, try to ask for praise from others.

Finding your own strategies to tackle your limiting beliefs is a really powerful way to help eliminate them. To achieve success, try to use the eleven steps below.

1   Recognise that you have a limiting belief.
2   Admit that it is a problem and that it limits you.
3   Resolve to tackle it.
4   Find strategies to overcome it – one step at a time. Get help to do this if you need to.
5   Employ the strategies deliberately.

6 Focus on what is and is not working, and use the strategies that produce most change.
7 Put in the time and effort necessary.
8 Get feedback from someone else, if possible.
9 Act on the feedback. Go back to step 4 if necessary.
10 Be prepared for others to mock you. Reframe your belief and use it to strengthen your resolve.
11 Praise yourself for progress and seek out praise from others. Use it to strengthen your resolve.

To grow is to learn

Your limiting beliefs can create a hypothetical comfort zone around you – a zone in which you are relaxed and comfortable because you don't feel stretched, stressed or pressured. While it's nice to feel this way, continually operating within your comfort zone will limit and eventually define you. You could end up being a person about which others say 'It's no good asking him. He never does anything different' or 'She's so predictable and boring – she never tries anything new.'

If you want to get better at something or rise to a challenge, you will have to grow and change. You will have to do something new and different. This will involve learning – learning how to adapt, and learning how to transfer your existing skills to new areas of life.

To do this you have to get out of your comfort zone and into the unknown – the growth zone (see Figure 5.1). The thought of doing this can make lots of people feel intimidated or even afraid because, suddenly, they realise that there is a high chance of failure, even of public humiliation. This can bring on feelings of pressure and stress, and is why many people abandon challenges and retreat to 'sticking with what they know'. They rationalise this by saying things like 'Better safe than sorry', 'Why take a chance?' 'Better the devil you know' or by blaming other factors which they see as beyond their control.

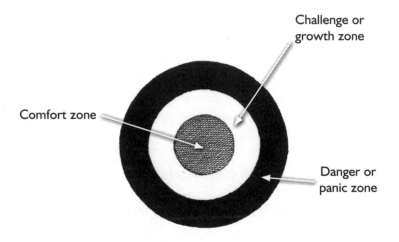

Challenge or growth zone

Comfort zone

Danger or panic zone

Figure 5.1: The zones.

People who habitually think like this not only limit their opportunities for growth, but they also, very likely, limit their chances for happiness. We are often at our happiest when we learn to get better at something, to overcome and master challenges, and when we get a great buzz from having done so.

Grow your comfort zone

The less you venture into the growth zone, the smaller your comfort zone will become. Negative beliefs tend to multiply and support each other. The consequence is an increasingly negative self-image. 'The less you do, the less you can do' as the saying goes. On the other hand, taking one small step every day towards your target will soon add up.

Sometimes, without you even realising, you will find you are more willing to try new things, go to new places, and make deeper, more personal contact with others. You discover that 'The more you do, the more you can do.'

Why are some people happy, successful and resilient? Because they are willing to be open-minded, resourceful and brave enough to learn, and to accept the risk of 'failure'. They know that they will often make mistakes and that learning from them and moving on are essential for growth. They are willing to look on others as role models, are open to advice, and they take and act upon feedback. They also feel that there is nothing quite as rewarding as making progress in something that is genuinely difficult. They understand that 'If you don't use it, you lose it' and that learning sets up new neural pathways in the brain. Carol Dweck's extensive research on this topic in her book *Mindset: The psychology of success*, shows us clearly the difference that a belief in learning can make to fulfilling your potential in life.

Developing a growth mindset

When Dweck began her research she was fascinated by why some children performed well and why others, despite having a high IQ, plateaued. She also worked with adults, discovering again and again that when it came to predicting their success over time, the way people think about their learning and what they believe about their ability is far more important than their IQ or exam results.

Dweck's experiments demonstrated how damaging limiting beliefs about intelligence can be. She took 330 students aged 11 and 12 and gave them a questionnaire to investigate their beliefs about intelligence. Those who believed their intelligence and personal qualities were set in stone had what Dweck called a *fixed* mindset. Those who believed that intelligence could be transformed through effort and that change is possible had what she called a *growth* mindset. She then gave the children a series of problems to solve, ranging from easy to difficult.

When the group with a fixed mindset came up against tough problems they couldn't do, they blamed their lack of intelligence, saying things like, 'I'm not very good at things like this' and 'I never did have a good memory.' As Dweck says, 'What was so striking about this was that only moments before, these students had a string of unbroken successes. Their intelligence and memory were working just fine.'[4] Their lack of faith in their ability was prompted when they started to struggle and became conscious of their incompetence. Their performance deteriorated and they became less effective at finding strategies or solutions that worked.

So how did the children with a growth mindset fare? When they came up against tough problems they tried new strategies, and some of them even solved problems that were considered beyond them. *They didn't believe that finding a question hard or getting something wrong was a symptom of failure.*

The gap in performance between the two groups was a result of their beliefs. Dweck found that this was true for adults just as much as it was for children. People with a growth mindset believe they can grow their intelligence though hard work, and that 'the hand you are dealt is just the starting point for development.'[5]

Many people with a fixed mindset don't really want feedback, especially if it's negative. They would prefer to ignore it rather than make the necessary changes. Think of the last time someone gave you constructive criticism. How did you feel? Did you feel that there was room for you to improve, or did you dismiss it? People with a fixed mindset may see that there is some truth in the feedback, but if they

---

4   C. Dweck, *Self-theories: Their role in motivation, personality, and development* (New York: Psychology Press, 2000), p. 7.
5   Dweck, *Mindset*, p. 7.

tried to change, they might fail and this would undermine their self-belief.

This can be especially true of some high-flyers at school or in work whose confidence, despite outward appearances, is often fragile. High-flyers can feel threatened by the success of others, instead of being inspired by them. Being top of the class from an early age or rising quickly at work can, naturally, feel really good. They feel that they are the cleverest in class or the most successful in work. This status becomes important to them, and they focus on continuing to prove how clever they are. To maintain this position, they might only take on easier challenges, which they know they can succeed at, and which allow them to continue cruising along within their comfort zone. They tend not to take on more stretching 'growth zone' challenges which they could fail at or, worse still, be seen by others to fail at. The result is that they could be in danger of plateauing – stopping growing.

When you think you are absolutely right, think again.

If someone has a fixed mindset then, when they are faced with a major challenge, they may not have the strategies in place to deal with getting things wrong or with personal failure. And they certainly don't want to lose face by having others see them struggle, so they tend not to seek help. Even if they do, they can come to see any constructive criticism as a threat, not as an opportunity to improve. They will defend their right not to change or grow, to stay right where they are, doing things the way they have always done them – even if it means that they miss out on chances of further success or happiness. Figure 5.2 summarises the features of fixed and growth mindsets.

Fixed mindset	Growth mindset
Intelligence is a given	Intelligence can grow
Leads to a desire to want to look smart and therefore develops a tendency to:	*Leads to a desire to want to learn and therefore develops a tendency to:*
Avoid challenges as can't risk failing	Embrace challenges willingly
Get defensive or give up too easily	Persist in the face of setbacks
See effort as fruitless or a sign of weakness	See effort as the path to mastery
Ignore useful negative feedback	Learn from criticism and welcome feedback
Feel threatened by the success of others, leading to fragile self-confidence and relentless perfectionism	Find lessons and inspiration in the success of others
As a result, may plateau early and not achieve potential	As a result, can reach ever higher levels of achievement

Figure 5.2: Features of fixed and growth mindsets.

You can always change your mindset

Do you have fixed mindset moments? As mentioned earlier, people with a fixed mindset can feel threatened by the success of others. They can go on to resent them and see others' success as a threat to their own self-esteem. Suppose you find out that a friend has got a fabulous new well-paid job or has passed a highly challenging academic course with distinction. What are your first thoughts? Are you jealous? Do you feel somehow demeaned by your friend's success? When you go to reunions, do you compare yourself with others and secretly hope they haven't reached the top of the career tree? Do you ever check Facebook and feel as though everyone else has a more exciting social life than you? Do you wonder how they did it, and why you can't?

If any of these apply to you, think on purpose about your reaction. Examine your reasons for your thinking. Is it jealousy or envy that is driving your reaction? Ask yourself, are these feelings going to make you feel happier or help you grow? Wouldn't it feel better to celebrate the success of others and, crucially, sit down and work out what the secrets of their success might be? If you can learn from the success of others, you will grow.

Do you seek others out and ask for their advice? Do you actively listen to their feedback and act on it? The growth mindset reaction to feedback is to welcome it and even willingly seek it, because you realise that it is challenging you to change. You feel that it shows that there might be a better way, and when you develop new skills and strategies to meet the challenge you grow. Feedback, as the old adage goes, is the breakfast of champions. Deliberately thinking like this will change your mindset.

In her book, Dweck tells the story of Nadja Salerno-Sonnenberg, a brilliant violinist who attended the world-famous Juilliard School to study with the famous violin teacher Dorothy DeLay. Unfortunately, Nadja had developed some bad habits in her playing which she was reluctant to change. As the years went by, other budding violinists made more progress than she did, and Nadja had a crisis of confidence. She became afraid of trying – and failing. She began to think that, if she didn't try, she had an excuse to fail. So she stopped bringing her violin to lessons. It became better not to try, than to try and fail. Even though she was an amazingly talented musician, she couldn't accept constructive criticism and that mindset halted her progress.

Here is a story about a bright boy who didn't like the feeling of failure.

Jeff was on the 'gifted and talented' register at school. He left with the expected A*s for GCSE and A levels and gained a place to study science at a top university. He was also talented at sport, and played rugby for his school and went on to play for the university team. This made him popular, and attracted a selection of prospective girlfriends. His older brother, Martin, on the other hand, was a middling student who got average grades at school. When he left, he got a good job and enjoyed life, with his sense of fun and light-hearted attitude.

By the middle of his first year at university, Jeff was struggling to balance his busy social and sporting life and keep up his studies for the first-class honours degree he was determined to get. He didn't like to tell his parents he was struggling, because he had never had to admit to this before, and he believed that if he did they would be disappointed in him. He struggled through the rest of his first year, becoming more and more desperate to succeed but avoiding tutorials and not asking for help.

Before his first year results came out, Jeff went home and his father took him and Martin out to play golf. The brothers hadn't played before. Martin was a natural, driving the ball smoothly off the first tee, sending it directly towards the hole. Over the next three holes Martin seemed to get better, but Jeff repeatedly missed or sliced the ball into the sand or water. Disgusted with himself, Jeff threw his clubs down and stormed off the course, shouting that it was an old man's game.

Later that summer, Jeff found out he had failed his first year. He left university, depressed by the setback and his disappointment in himself. During this time, he became interested in psychology and read about mindsets, motivation and resilience. This helped him reflect on how he could reignite his love of learning and make the most of his ability. It took two years for him to recover from his depression before he could bring himself to start another university course.

We are all vulnerable to these types of feelings. Recognising them, understanding them and trying to challenge them is essential if we want to manage our moods and emotions more effectively. The secret of being able to grow is to be able to avoid habitual fixed mindset responses and be open to new ways of looking at situations. This is an ongoing challenge for us all.

Imagine the following scenario. What would your reaction be? You have had an appraisal at work and are told that an aspect of your performance is not satisfactory. On your way home you get caught by a speed camera and when you get home your partner has to rush out to a meeting and is too busy to listen to your woes, leaving you to brood on the day's events alone.

The fixed mindset response would be to think that what happens in our lives defines us and that there is little we, or anyone else, can do to change it. Fixed mindset negative reactions to these events might be to say, 'I feel like I'm a failure', 'I'm no good at my job', 'This is typical of my luck' or 'My partner doesn't care'. As a result, the future looks bleak and you might sulk or to feel that all is lost. Some people with a fixed mindset might also react by saying things such as, 'The appraisers didn't know what they were talking about' or 'Stupid place to put a speed camera' to (wrongly) justify their thinking.

This response is a habitual leap to a negative interpretation of these discouraging, but not irremediable, events, – which goes on to reinforce negative self-beliefs. Thankfully, it is rare to find a person who has a fixed mindset about everything, or to find someone who never has a fixed mindset about anything.

It is important to think on purpose about your reaction to events. As soon as fixed mindset beliefs kick in, immediately try to recognise how you are feeling, why this is, and then understand where this think-ing could take you. When we feel ourselves responding negatively to events, it is time to reframe our thinking and consider how thinking differently could lead to a better outcome.

You could try to think of growth mindset responses to the earlier scenario, such as:

'Wow! I'm glad my appraisers mentioned I need to improve my performance there. I hadn't realised people saw me like that. I need to get some feedback from my team and from other colleagues about what I can do to improve.'

'I need to slow down, pay attention and stick to the speed limit in future. The speed camera is there for a reason.'

'I wonder if my partner is feeling stressed at the moment? I'll ask when he gets back.'

These reframe the same events in a more positive and productive light. Sometimes it is also useful not to have a fixed mindset belief that the magic bullet for all situations is to have a growth mindset! There are times when having a fixed mindset can be an advantage – for example, when you are standing up for your rights or for something you believe in. A fixed mindset can also help support you to be determined and clear in your goals. The secret is to recognise when a fixed mindset is holding you back and then to be able to tweak your thinking to be open to change.

Remember that mindset theory (like any other theories and the advice in this book) is useful for certain contexts. We need to be flexible when we apply any personal development theory to our own circumstances. When you read about the latest theory, always take a step back, reflect on it, and think about whether it can work for you.

Find out more about your mindset

Here is a quiz based on Carol Dweck's explanation of the attitudes required to develop a growth mindset.

Mindset checkout

Score yourself from 1–4 in answer to each question, where 1 = always, 2 = often, 3 = sometimes, 4 = rarely.

Do you ...	1 to 4
Believe intelligence can be learned?	
Always see mistakes as learning opportunities?	
Enjoy new challenges and feel comfortable with change?	
Know how you learn best?	

Do you ...	1 to 4
Enjoy a challenge where you have to make maximum effort?	
Ask for help when you need it?	
Try out new things every day?	
Feel comfortable meeting new people?	
Have a list of new hobbies you would like to try?	
Know how to motivate yourself to work hard when you need to?	
Go to places on your own?	
Review your goals regularly?	
Find change easy to manage?	
Get inspired when other people enjoy success, and learn from them?	
Enjoy a wide range of fiction and non-fiction reading?	
Enjoy a good philosophical or political discussion with others with a range of views?	
Change your mind and views?	
Get asked for your advice and guidance by friends and family?	
Like to try new activities, places, films and food as often as possible?	
Consider yourself to be a learner above everything else?	

Add up your scores. The lower your score, the more of a growth mindset you have.
Total ....

Look carefully at the questions which you scored 3 or 4, as these represent your fixed mindset answers. Set yourself a couple of targets to work on this year that relate to those questions. Write them down below.

Targets:

Addicted to success

It is ironic that success can lead to fragile self-confidence. You would think that, the more successful you are, the more confident you become. It seems logical. We first learn how good it is to get positive feedback as small children. It makes us feel great to be told we have done well, or hear how clever we have been.

Praise can be a real problem, however. We have all received and enjoyed well-meant praise at one time or another for something we have produced or done. If continually producing a praiseworthy product becomes our claim to fame, this can become counter-productive. It can lead to us becoming addicted to getting things right – as opposed to taking risks, making mistakes and learning.

This has implications for bright, capable people. Imagine you are awarded the 'Employee of the Month' prize. Next time, when someone else gets it and you don't, how does that make you feel? Sustaining peak performance is tough, especially if it is dependent on factors that are beyond our control, as most success is. If you believe your identity is firmly chained to your performance outcomes, then success can become a burden. We can begin to feel that we continually have to live up to our past triumphs. Whether these are exam results or sales targets, obsessing over measuring yourself by outcome can lead to a reluctance to challenge yourself with difficult tasks, as these risk failure.

When you are out of your depth, you learn to swim or die.

A belief in the power of effort and prioritising the process learning (above just getting it right) will give us all a chance to grow new neural pathways. Dweck's research has shown that long-term success comes to those who believe that the challenge to learn was their motivation: that the struggle to learn should be relished and making mistakes seen as an opportunity.

If learning means making mistakes, it also might make you feel incompetent. Have you got what it takes to overcome this? Think of when you learned to drive. Even your parents could do it. It seemed like such a simple thing to do – before you started learning how! In your state of unconscious incompetence you had no idea what was waiting for you. Then, when you took your first lessons, the realisation dawned that this was really, really hard. You instantly became consciously incompetent. There's so much to think about – gear changes, clutch control, steering, braking, checking the road ahead, checking your mirrors, watching out for other road users. The thought that it could be very expensive if things went wrong. Worse, that your mistakes could be dangerous – or even fatal – to you and to others.

This is when some people, after a short period of trying, develop limiting beliefs and think they will never master being able to drive. Some think catastrophically and imagine that they may kill themselves or others, then give up. They may justify this by concocting excuses or conjuring up limiting beliefs such as 'The instructor was rubbish', 'This is too hard', I'm useless at this' or 'I didn't want to do it anyway.'

It can take years for some people to rebuild their motivation, confidence and determination to try again. Others may have learned to take and act upon feedback. This will help you endure the hard graft and hours of practice needed to get through the stage of conscious competence. Do you remember consciously and deliberately checking your mirrors, learning clutch control when starting off (especially uphill, with cars just behind you), and learning the myriad other skills needed to drive? Would you have thought that some years later you could drive effortlessly for miles without consciously rehearsing every manoeuvre? This is when you realise that all the effort and practice has paid off, and that you have become unconsciously competent.

When we have the opportunity to learn anything new – a foreign language, bungee jumping, a musical instrument, some new computer software or app, or extra responsibilities at work – we suddenly become conscious of our incompetence. At this point we have a choice. We can panic and start having negative thoughts about the challenges ahead of us, and decide not to bother. If we let opportunities pass and allow ourselves to slip back into our comfort zone, we miss out on new experiences and often look back on these missed opportunities with regret. But, even more importantly, people who habitually do this do not grow.

On the other hand, we can think on purpose and examine and challenge our negative beliefs. We can turn them into bite-sized chunks which we can deal with one at a time. This helps us to find the resolve and motivation we need to develop a set of positive beliefs which say 'This is a challenge worth doing and which I can do. I'm ready for the hard work, because this is how I grow.'

With practice, you can get to the stage where you can just say, 'OK, this is just another challenge' and get on with it, knowing that you have the resources and have built up a reservoir of experience to cope with most things. Also, you know that if you get stuck, all you have to do is ask for help. No big deal!

Your courage, creativity and flexibility are going to be all-important if you are to move through the next stage of conscious competence. Here you are, in a hard place, where you are aware that you really do have a lot to learn and that you will need the (10,000) hours of practice to be able to master the challenge.

The path to excellence ... is steep and gruelling and arduous. It is inordinately lengthy, requiring a minimum of 10,000 hours of lung-busting effort to get to the summit. And most important of all, it forces voyagers to stumble and fall on every single stretch of the journey.

Matthew Syed[6]

This is where the eleven steps to overcoming limiting beliefs (see p. 120) come into play. When you're consciously incompetent, keep your long-term aim in mind. Above all, remember that you are still on a journey to growth. If your fingers won't stretch to play those

---

6 Syed, *Bounce*, p. 120.

awkward piano notes, if you are struggling with basic words and phrases in a foreign language, or if you are in unfamiliar territory at work, remember that success is possible with grit and determination. It may take hours of practice. You may need to write down all the instructions. You will have to take advice and act on feedback but eventually, as practice makes perfect, new skills start to become automatic.

Choose to grow

With practice, your newly learned skills will become fully honed and you will become unconsciously competent in them. They become part of what you do, either at work or at play – they become your habitual behaviour. As we have seen, people who choose to grow see every change or challenge as an opportunity, and mistakes as a useful chance to learn more. If you think on purpose and deliberately grow this sort of attitude you will have more flexibility and a wider range of strategies to choose from when life tests you. This means that you will be more likely to respond to change – and challenge – successfully, thus contributing to your success and happiness.

Reflect and review

- Your beliefs and values matter – check out Chapter 3 to remind yourself about your personal shield of values.
- Our beliefs can be limiting, and can influence our attitudes and behaviour without us realising it.
- Limiting beliefs create thoughts that can get in the way of success and happiness.
- Phobias can develop from limiting beliefs.

- Reframing your beliefs can help to change your outcomes and overcome fears.
- Pushing yourself outside your comfort zone, regularly, gives you the courage to take risks.
- Purposeful practice is more important than innate talent.
- You need courage and flexibility to rewire your brain and become better at consciously growing your mindset.
- Carol Dweck found that people with a fixed mindset had limiting beliefs that may restrict their ability to fulfil their potential.
- Alternatively, developing a growth mindset means believing your intelligence and your personal qualities can change and grow over time.

Points of view

Q Whatever you say about intelligence not being fixed, I am afraid it is obvious that some people are cleverer than others. I have evidence of this in my own family. One of my sons has struggled academically since primary school, and my other son has been gifted from the beginning. I'm convinced we are born with a certain IQ, and any changes during our lifetime are pretty superficial.

All this focus on effort is very misleading (and cruel) for children who will never have the ability to pass exams, no matter how hard they try. What about children with special educational needs? Can they really develop a growth mindset and achieve? Some of them find it hard to even write their names. Please spare me the fake optimism and face the fact that bright kids will succeed and dim kids will struggle. Someone has to stack shelves!

A You make some very valid points about the differences we see in children's abilities, and I agree that we have to avoid giving people false expectations that will lead to disappointment. When we are thinking about fulfilling our personal potential, it may be better to think that we all have a starting point – which will be different for each of us – and effort can help us make more of that potential.

Have you ever known anyone who has surprised you by what they have achieved? As a teacher, I knew a student who had special needs. The school forecast that he would be unable to attain any GCSE grades above a G, but he went on to become a great success in a gardening business, eventually becoming a well-paid director.

Have you known people who have a high IQ and got great exam results, but have not been able to fulfil that early promise later on in work and life? High IQ is not necessarily a predictor of success. There are other important factors, such as determination, self-regulation and empathy. Having a growth mindset fosters these. Developing a growth mindset means becoming the best learner you can be – whatever brain you have been born with. It includes finding out what your passions are, what motivates you, and how your brain works best.

Whatever your age or ability, you can still try to learn new things and new ways of thinking. There is evidence that, if you believe this, you will achieve more. Or you can believe intelligence is fixed and we are what we are. It's up to you!

Chapter 6

Thinking on purpose

How to deliberately change your mind

Thinking on purpose means taking control of what goes on in your head and changing it if you need to. We have seen how a knowledge of the three-part brain helps us to understand our thinking and control the primitive reptilian brain. This chapter reviews some of the ideas discussed earlier, and develops them to show you how to more easily 'think on purpose' so that you become as cognitively flexible as you need to be in order to change and grow.

How thinking works

In his fascinating book *Thinking, Fast and Slow* Daniel Kahneman shows us how automatic our thinking is by asking the reader to look at a photograph like this: (see Figure 6.1).[1]

Figure 6.1: How do you react to this picture?

I   Kahneman, *Thinking, Fast and Slow*, p. 22.

You see an angry man pointing at you, about to say something unpleasant in a loud voice. This premonition came into your mind without effort or any deliberate intention. Your thinking was automatic and intuitive – or what Kahneman calls 'fast thinking'. You later see that he is also balding.

Now think about this question: in what situations might the behaviour shown in this picture be acceptable? (Don't go on to read the next paragraph until you have done this.)

Done? Now, think about your thinking. Did it go something like this?

To answer the question you first have to recognise the man's expression, define the emotions this represents, and then search your memory banks for examples of such behaviour. You next reference these memories against the beliefs you have about what this behaviour means to you, and check how these memories made you feel at the time. Only then do you go on to assess the ethical and moral aspects of the various situations where someone may have this expression and, finally, start to formulate a reasoned, balanced argument which answers the question. This is what Kahneman calls 'slow' thinking. Whereas 'fast' thinking was effortless, the 'slow' thinking task required purposeful thinking and concentration.

You need 'slow' thinking when you are trying to remember rarely used names and phone numbers, reverse into a parking space, or when you are employing any other rarely used skill. Exceptions are things like dialling a phone number you use often. Because you have rung it so many times, you can automatically relate a string of otherwise meaningless numbers to a name.

'Slow' thinking is what happens when we are in the 'conscious competence' stage discussed in Chapter 5, but it can also become an unconscious habit, with practice. For example, some of you may be great at mental arithmetic and know that 13×14 is (without having to put in any effort) 182.

Our 'fast thinking' automatic pilot is very useful and saves us time and effort. Some basic functions (such as digesting our food, or breathing) are, thankfully, run automatically by our reptilian brain, but functions that are dealt with by the thinking brain can also become automatic.

Running on automatic pilot can be useful, but can also be detrimental. If we are driving, miles may pass as we cruise along the motorway, perhaps listening to music, without us really thinking about driving or what we are doing. Then a police car appears in the rear-view mirror and 'slow' thinking takes over, making us focus. We check our speed and move carefully and deliberately out of the way.

At a party you might be automatically gliding through the room, drawing conclusions about the ages, social status and intelligence of the people around you, when suddenly you hear a fire alarm. Your 'slow thinking' kicks into action to consider the otherwise unnoticed exit opportunities. In each case you have been jerked out of your automatic fast thinking state into assessing and re-evaluating the situation you are in.

If we want to manage the way we think, we have to recognise that efficient fast thinking can lead to us having fixed, automatic attitudes to events in life and certain habitual ways of thinking. We may have formed opinions or attitudes about ourselves or others and never really examined them. You might think, 'I don't get on with rugby players' but is this fair, correct in all cases, or helpful? We really need to challenge unconscious fixed attitudes such as these by thinking on purpose.

Thinking on purpose means developing the ability to pause, stand back and look at whether 'fast thinking' is going to give you the best possible outcome.

'Fast' versus 'slow' thinking

Which thinking system is more powerful and important to us? Slow thinking involves a lot of concentration, as we consciously make choices and search our memories and belief systems for evidence about what to do next. This can absorb almost all our attention, so that when we are in 'slow' thinking mode, we can become effectively blind to the obvious.

This has been shown several times, including in a classic experiment in which viewers were asked to count the number of basketball passes in a film.[2] During the game a woman wearing a gorilla suit appears in full view of the camera for nine seconds, during which she crosses the court and thumps her chest. Amazingly, half of the people who viewed the film did not see the gorilla. And these people, when asked about it later, refuse to believe the gorilla was ever there. As Kahneman stresses, this type of example shows we can be 'blind to the obvious and blind to our blindness'.[3] We can't always believe what we see, or what we think we see, or even believe what we think.

On the other hand, fast thinking is *so* fast that it seems to be out of our control – but it is important. 'Fast' thinking simply short-circuits all the deliberation that 'slow' thinking uses, and it runs the show most of the time. This is how we are able to come up with immediate conclusions, rightly or wrongly, about what is happening around us. Also, very significantly, the impressions and instinctive reactions which 'fast' thinking feeds us, percolate into our 'slow' thinking.

This is important because, over time, this can alter the way that 'slow' thinking creates beliefs and actions. It can lead to us making unthinking over-generalisations about events or people, and lead to

---

2   C. Chabris and D. Simons, 'The Invisible Gorilla' [video]. Available at: www. theinvisiblegorilla.com/gorilla_experiment.html.

3   Kahneman, *Thinking, Fast and Slow*, p. 24.

us saying thoughtless things. When we do this we don't notice until afterwards that what we have said or done has resulted in distress. Do you ever find yourself having to apologise, saying 'I didn't mean to upset you', 'I was only joking' or 'I didn't realise you were feeling like that'? If you do, it is probably because you have been relying too much on your 'fast' thinking and have not been thinking on purpose.

Even more importantly, the slow percolation of impressions and instinctive reactions from our 'fast' thinking into our 'slow' thinking can alter our default setting of happiness. When this is combined with our ingrained negativity bias (discussed in Chapter 2), we can begin to see the glass as always half-empty, never half-full. We see and dwell on the misery in the world and on the negative events in our lives, rather than the opposite. We can end up with a default setting of unhappiness and dissatisfaction, and this can affect how we interact with others and see the world.

What you think and do can too often originate in your 'fast' thinking unconscious mind, but it is your conscious mind that allows you to rationalise, take control and make the best choices. For example, it is 'slow' thinking which prevents uncontrollable anger. It stops you losing your temper in a queue in the bank, or throwing your computer at the wall when it crashes. If we think on purpose we can make deliberate decisions to choose feelings, take part in activities, and use strategies for interacting with others that will make us happier.

By using metacognition to stand back from and understand what your 'fast' thinking is saying, you allow room to think on purpose about the best outcome. You can reflect on whether the beliefs your intuition is acting on are still valid and useful for you. Are all men in uniform really sexist? Are all single parents feckless? Is rain always depressing? Are you incapable of jumping out of a plane in a parachute, or speaking up against a bully at work?

Our intuitive 'fast' thinking is also closely linked with the primitive brain and the hormonal and physical reactions we feel. For example, 'fast' thinking can automatically associate flying with fear, and make your heart beat too fast on take-off. It can stop you speaking up and contributing to an important work meeting because it immediately defaults to mantras like 'I might sound stupid' or 'I can't do this'. 'Fast' thinking can make you instinctively mean or generous – no matter what your financial status, as the example below shows.

James's story

James grew up in a family where money was tight. There was little pocket money or spare cash for holidays or school trips. He noticed that the arrival of a bank statement always created tension and arguments between his parents. As he got older James learned to save up his meagre pocket money to buy decent train-ers or other treats. He took on countless part-time jobs, always eager to make a penny or two. He took very good care of every penny he earned, as he knew the effort it took to make it.

Fast forward twenty years. James now found himself with more money than he could ever have dreamed of. His entrepre-neurial streak had led him to start his own business in his twenties. Hard work, shrewd use of his resources, and a touch of daring led him to make a breakthrough, providing a technical service that everyone seemed to want.

The future looked bright, but James couldn't shake off his default setting. He was still careful with money. He still felt instinctively that spending on what he saw as luxuries was frivo-lous, so he lived in a modest flat and drove an ancient, but reliable, car. Fashion didn't interest him so his clothes tended to be worn for a long time. Out with friends, he usually had to be reminded to get a round in at the pub. He started to get a reputation as a bit of a miser but, no matter how much money he had, he still acted on his ingrained instinct or default setting – to save and hoard.

Should James change? If so, could he alter his thinking to take account of his present circumstances and enjoy his money? What would it take to change James and his attitude to money?

The first step could be for him to think on purpose, to use the process of metacognition and self-awareness and to seek feedback on his behaviour from a trusted friend. Then later, when he thinks about buying a new car or taking the family on a special holiday, even though his instinct is shouting, 'It's wasteful, too expensive or unnecessary!' he could pause and purposefully think, 'I can now afford it.' Eventually, he could learn to recognise his instinctive responses, smile at them, assess and evaluate them, and habitually take control of his thinking so that he gets the outcomes he wants. If he did this for long enough, his beliefs about money would change.

Of course there is nothing wrong with continuing to be who you are – or to have the personality your default setting defines for you. If it is working for you, it is powerful and useful. When it stops working for you, try thinking in a different way.

The following example relates to parenting.

Wendy's story

Wendy was a pretty little girl whose gorgeous brown curly hair and blue eyes always got attention. However, she had always struggled with her reading at school and hated being bottom of the class in tests. Even when she eventually learned to write she found it hard to think of stories and was always more interested in watching TV than doing homework. Her older sister, on the other hand, was a bright spark and seemed to pick things up very quickly and, to Wendy's envy, was the apple of her mother's eye.

By the time Wendy was fourteen, she was a favourite with the boys and loved being the most popular choice as a dance partner at the annual school ballroom dancing competition. By sixteen, she had failed her exams at school but was even more popular with the boys. At eighteen she got engaged and married to the first man who proposed to her. When she got pregnant and had her first child later that year, being at home as a mother and housewife seemed a far better choice than working in a low-paid job. Her first baby, when it was so dependent on her, made her feel so loved and needed that she had another, and another, and another … It didn't matter that it was hard to make ends meet and that she didn't seem to have any hope of having a career. Benefits helped, and because each baby loved her more than anything in the world, it was worth it. Wendy was instinctively seeking out unconditional love to plug the gap in her self-esteem – and it was working.

As her babies grew up, they became rebellious toddlers, then older children, and Wendy found them harder to love. Nevertheless, she still had a basic need for love, so she carried on having babies and also began to collect animals, especially dogs, because they loved her unconditionally. People would ask her why she had so many children, and now also all the dogs, but all she could say was that they made her happy. Sometimes she felt others were criticising her lifestyle. If so, her instinct was to lash out with anger and venom, saying things like, 'What's it to you? If I want more babies and animals, I'll have them. I deserve to be happy – why shouldn't I?'

Meanwhile, one of her daughters is a pretty little thing who struggles with literacy. Her older sister, on the other hand, is a bright spark and seems to pick things up very quickly …

We have all seen people like Wendy playing out the scripts written for them in childhood, living on benefits or appearing on TV programmes like *The Jeremy Kyle Show*. They are sure that their instincts are reliable, and have extremely fixed mindsets which justify their way of life. No amount of logic will help Wendy change her mind about why it isn't wise to have more dogs or babies. Her instinctive need for love and acknowledgement is fulfilled by her default-setting choices. So does she really have a choice? Her husband has learnt to placate her for an easy life. She may even have chosen him for this reason.

Self-regulation

Could Wendy think on purpose and have more control over her impulsive actions? There is some evidence that teaching young people to self-regulate through metacognition substantially improves their achievements,[4] but what exactly is self-regulation, and how important is it for success and happiness? Self-regulation is emotional self-control, and Daniel Goleman says it 'may require a special effort at first' to make it a habit.[5] He stresses that managing emotional impulses is 'real mental work' and creates new neural pathways that need to be strengthened over time and with practice.

Self-regulation begins when we are toddlers, with the first time we can't do or get exactly what we want, so we throw our first frustrated tantrum. Most of us grow up and learn that we often have to have patience and defer our gratification: to put off having something good now, in the expectation of getting something even better later. But

4   S. Higgins et al., The Sutton Trust-Education Endowment Foundation Teaching and Learning Toolkit (London: Education Endowment Foundation, 2014). Available at: https://educationendowmentfoundation.org.uk/evidence/teaching-learning-toolkit/meta-cognition-and-self-regulation/.

5   D. Goleman, *The New Leaders* (London: Time Warner, 2002), p. 203.

some of us find this very hard to do. The famous marshmallow test, mentioned by Goleman in his first book, shows that the ability to control desires is demonstrable from a young age.[6] Children as young as five were placed in a room, given a marshmallow and told that they could eat it now – or wait fifteen minutes and receive two. The researchers tracked these children over the rest of their lives and made some very surprising discoveries.

They found that children who could wait and defer their gratification went on to achieve better results at school and in work. They also had longer-lasting relationships and were less likely to suffer from drug and alcohol addiction. The deferrers also had lower body mass indexes as adults than those who couldn't resist temptation. Although others have since debunked some of the conclusions of this study, a very recent, similar test with very young children revealed interesting results. The toddlers were offered a raisin which was hidden underneath a cup. They were asked not to eat it for 60 seconds, then they were told they could. The researchers found that those who took the raisin before getting permission were more likely to have problems at school later. The test seemed to predict a child's future impulsiveness, attention and learning capacity seven years later.[7] Early interventions to help children like these develop self-regulation skills could have a powerful impact on future outcomes.

Why is this? Are the deferrers somehow able to make better life choices? Are their 'fast' thinking instincts helping, or preventing them from self-regulating? Do they somehow use 'slow' thinking to avoid a life affected by impulsive bad choices, relationship breakdowns, emotional outbursts and self-destructive behaviours? Or does the answer

---

6   D. Goleman, *Emotional Intelligence*: why it matters more than IQ (London: Bloomsbury, 2004), p. 80.

7   See J. Jaekel, S. Eryigit-Madzwamuse and D. Wolke, 'Preterm Toddlers' Inhibitory Control Abilities Predict Attention Regulation and Academic Achievement at Age 8 Years', *Journal of Pediatrics* (February 2016) 169: 87–92.

lie in what psychologists call cognitive control – the ability to choose to adapt your behaviour to pursue a goal you set for yourself?

Having cognitive control involves a lot of work. You have to keep the goal in mind, not allow yourself to be distracted from it, and go on to set up, apply and sustain a strategy for achieving that goal. Then you have to monitor your actions to see if the goal is being achieved, and modify the strategy if it is not successful. To put it simply – you have to think on purpose.

It would appear that the deferrers learned to think purposefully at a young age and created neural pathways to allow them to do so. There is no reason why we cannot learn to do this as well, providing we have the motivation. And what can be more motivating than wanting to lead a happier and more successful life? Being able to think on purpose and defer our gratification is an essential long-term thinking skill for learning and, as we have seen, for living. In the short term, creating a space to think on purpose about our instinct to respond quickly and, instead, having a well-thought-out reaction could prevent hasty mistakes, road rage and temper tantrums.

Here is one mother's story.

Leg of Lamb

I discovered in a scary moment what a temper I had if, for one moment, I let the red mist cloud my judgement.

It was an ordinary Saturday morning. I had been shopping for groceries after a tough week at work. My husband was working in the garden. By the time I returned from shopping, my three young teenage daughters had just got up. One was in the shower, another was still in her room and the youngest, who was only twelve at the time, came into the kitchen. There was I, trying to unpack the shopping and put it away, while she, ignoring me, started getting breakfast. Something snapped.

I launched into a tirade, showing real anger that not only had I done all the shopping but now no one was helping me put it away. A veritable volcano of temper built up as I started shouting at her and slamming things down on the work surface. Finally, I picked up a big fat leg of lamb and threw it wildly across the room – at my youngest daughter! It missed her by inches, but her shock and fear at my sudden loss of control made her dissolve into tears. Still in a blind rage, I ignored her and stormed to the shower room. I started banging on the door, shouting at my daughter in there to come out, using language that no one had ever heard me say before. Next, I was screaming up the stairs to my third daughter, who was hiding in her bedroom. My language continued to stun the girls. I was on a roll – a roll of temper and emotion. I described all the reasons why I was sick of them, how I had to do everything for them, how I was taken for granted, unappreciated, etc. etc. It didn't end until all the girls were in tears and my shocked husband had come in from the garden to make the peace.

Thankfully, nothing like this had ever happened before – and has never happened since. With hindsight, I felt ashamed that I had let my resentment build up so much that I almost literally blew my top. However, I also noticed some other interesting things about the incident. There was a definite moment when I felt the red mist start to come down, when I could see my finger hovering over the nuclear button before I chose to press it. I discovered that pressing it, and losing my temper, was strangely satisfying and self-indulgent, as it allowed my pent-up, controlled emotions to explode. I also realised that, now that I'd done it once, it would be even easier to do it again.

Now I know I have that type of temper, I have developed

strategies for controlling it. I distract myself, think of something else, breathe deeply, or visualise the nuclear button being out of reach. Going ballistic, punching the wall, pouring out my rage and afterwards grabbing a gin and tonic or a cigarette may make me feel better initially, but in reality it is destructive and doesn't fix the root cause of the problem.

Happily, 'The day Mum threw a leg of lamb at me' is now the stuff of family legend, and is the only incident of its type.
'Just losing it' can become a dangerous habit. Some people even enjoy the fear it induces in others and mistake it for power. That can be the path to emotional or physical abuse, and leads to people around you having to tread carefully to prevent a tantrum.

I am ashamed to say the story above is my own. I didn't want my family to be afraid of my temper, so learning self-control was important. The secret is to keep in contact with your thoughts and feelings so that this type of explosion doesn't occur. It is hard work and takes commitment and energy to take control when you have been in the habit of losing it, but, of course, long-term mental health can benefit from mood regulation.[8]

Making the effort to exercise self-control or defer your gratification can also become a habit. With practice you can create new neural pathways that allow you to reflect and create that necessary thinking time between your impulse and action, so you make the right choices.

Do you:

- resist putting off that major project in the garden, decorating that room, or writing that novel?

---

8   For further information see A.M. Isen, Positive affect. In T. Dalgleish and M. Power (eds), *Handbook of Cognition and Emotion* (Chichester: John Wiley & Sons, 1999) pp. 521–540.

- resist the temptation to have that extra slice of cake or glass of wine?
- have a list of jobs and do the worst thing first, avoiding displacement activities such as checking your emails or watching TV?
- exercise regularly and make the effort to cook healthy meals?
- discipline yourself to listen more to those you love and give up some of your time to help someone else who needs help?

Our impulses can become automatic behaviours that can lead to bad habits. You can only choose the better path if you are in control of your thinking and so are able to resist your impulses.

Inertia – or the apathy habit that holds you back

Do you sometimes feel that time seems to have drifted by? Do you feel angry when you think about what you could have achieved, but haven't, because you somehow seem trapped by inertia or the fear of trying something new?

Keith's story

Keith had been working late every night. He would often arrive home with a takeaway and have a beer and a cigarette to help him relax. It seemed there was always so much work to do – there was no end to it. He hadn't been in touch with friends for a while because when he remembered to call them it was always too late in the evening. He felt exhausted at the weekends, so he sat around in his bedsit for most of Saturday, not bothering to dress, just watching TV or playing computer games. It was his reward for getting through another week. Meanwhile, he was watching his waistline get larger and his circle of friends get slowly smaller. When he went home for a family event, his mum mentioned how run-down he looked. She gently asked him why, and if he had met anyone significant yet. He snapped back at her that it was none of her business and the next day left as soon as possible.

On the train ride back to London he thought about the life he had been leading for the three years he had been there. The excitement of a big job in the city after university had become a treadmill of work. When he went out to the occasional social event he would watch everyone else enjoying their social life, laughing with friends or partners over a meal or after-work drinks. They would talk about the festivals and raves they had been to, the gyms and clubs they had joined, what their plans were for the weekend, who they were dating, and so on. Keith suddenly realised how much he listened and how little he *did*.

Glumly, he started to think things through. Why did everyone else seem to be having such a good time – the time he thought he was going to have – while life was passing him by as he sped towards the big 30? Should he give it up, go back to suburbia and marry the girl next door? Should he go travelling again and escape the drudgery? Should he look for another job? But jobs in his line of work were often similarly demanding, so would it be more of the same? Also, he would have to take the time to update his CV and anyway, when would he find the time to search for new jobs?

He arrived back at his bedsit with a nice takeaway, cracked open a can and watched a film. It wasn't so bad. Work was OK, really, and the money was alright. Something was bound to happen soon. Maybe he would meet someone nice at work, or one day move to a house share or maybe even sign up for internet dating … But meanwhile, he dozed off in front of the box.

Two years later, Keith is a little older, a little fatter, a little lonelier and a little more set in his ways.

Keith is suffering from inertia. He is finding it hard to make decisions and choices that would take him outside his comfort zone. He takes the path of least resistance, following his natural inclination to do what he has always done. That fixed mindset provides a comfy bubble of certainty. It is just too much effort or too scary to take a different path. Fears that he isn't really happy or achieving what he wants in life will frequently float into his mind, but if he wants things to change he will need to think differently and purposefully.

The definition of insanity is doing the same thing over and over again and expecting a different result.

How to take control and think on purpose

First, realise that you have a choice in what you do and how you react to situations. For example, believing in yourself is a choice. Being willing to take a risk is a choice. Being in a good mood that spreads happiness – or being irritable and spreading gloom – is a choice.

To make the choices that will make you happier, you need to be able to stand back from your own impulsive, ingrained, habitual reactions to situations – especially if they are of anger, sadness, grief, envy, greed, pride, fear or cynicism. If you don't, they will create inner dialogues like the following.

'I've had enough of this. I'm not standing for it.'
'It always happens to me. It's not fair.'
'I can't go on – it's just too hard.'
'I'm trapped and I just can't escape.'
'I don't deserve anything better.'
'Why should I bother?'
'She gets everything and I get nothing.'
'I deserve more money, clothes, friends, etc.'
'It might go horribly wrong.'
'People will laugh at me.'
'What if I can't do it?'
'It feels too scary to take a chance.'
'Most people are nasty and will laugh at me.'
'Everyone is luckier than me.'
'I can never forgive him.'
'It will never work.'
'I can't do it.'
'I won't do it.'

This type of inner dialogue can very easily become a habitual way of thinking and of seeing the world. But, worse than this, it becomes limiting because it prevents thoughts about choice, opportunity and growth. It replaces these with negative thoughts which, when repeated often enough, can become negative beliefs and self-fulfilling prophecies. Thinking on purpose means, first, that you recognise this is true and, second, that you challenge the thoughts, perhaps as shown in Table 6.1.

Table 6.1: Reframing thoughts.

Inner dialogue	Thinking on purpose
I've had enough of this. I'm not standing for it.	This is making feel angry. I need to chill and find a new way to look at it.
It always happens to me. It's not fair.	This has happened before, but let's think about how I can make sure it doesn't happen again.
I can't go on – it's just too hard.	It's really hard, but it is growing my resilience and my brain because I am learning so much.
I'm trapped and I just can't escape.	I can escape from this – I need to find a way out by asking for help.
I don't deserve anything better.	I deserve something better because I am trying my best.
Why should I bother?	If I bother then I will feel better about things.
She gets everything and I get nothing.	I'm glad she gets nice things, but I am lucky in other ways.
I deserve more money, clothes, friends, etc.	What I give is what I get.
It might go horribly wrong.	It might go right … and if it goes wrong I can deal with it.
People will laugh at me.	People may laugh, but I'm fine with that because I tried and that's what matters.

Inner dialogue	Thinking on purpose
What if I can't do it?	What if I *can* do it?
It feels too scary to take a chance.	I can feel scared, but that's OK because that means I have been brave enough to take a chance.
Most people are nasty and will laugh at me.	Lots of people are nice and will support me.
Everyone is luckier than me.	I can focus on the things that make me a lucky person too.
I can never forgive him.	I can move on and forgive him because hating him just makes me feel bad.
It will never work.	It could work – I will make it work.
I can't do it.	I *can* do it if …
I won't do it.	I *will* give it a try.

The negative inner dialogue that inhibits your success and happiness can become so habitual that you might not even be aware of it repeating inside your head. The self-evaluation quizzes in Chapter 3 are helpful for you to get to know how your thinking works. But to make thinking on purpose a habit, you first have to build it into your belief system. You have to believe that change can happen and that thinking so makes a difference. This will give you the motivation to consciously change your thinking patterns so that they work to give you the outcomes you want.

It is sometimes very hard to challenge your habitual reactions to situations and so avoid the emotions they make you feel. It is hard, too, to challenge your limiting beliefs. After all, it is these reactions, emotions and beliefs that have dictated your thinking, perhaps for many years. They have excused your past behaviour, and made it easier for you to avoid trying new things and fall back on bad habits. You have to be able to mentally stand back, think about your habitual, impulsive reaction and see if it is preventing you from growing. If it is, then think about how to get the outcome you want.

Focus on the outcome you want

Our beliefs – as discussed in Chapter 5 – help us get clarity about the outcome that we want from any situation. So often, events happen and we react to them without thinking. It is the reaction that creates the problems. Always make time to *pause* and think about the outcome you want from the situation.

For example, your neighbour has started behaving in an unacceptable manner. He has been parking in front of your drive, playing loud music in the garden, cutting back branches from your apple tree, and now you suspect that he may be poisoning your cat. You can choose to go round to his house, lose your temper, tell him what you think and threaten him with retribution and legal action. He responds in kind, even more loudly, and tells you where to put your threats. Then the war begins – a war of attrition that you didn't want and now have to live with every day. You still have to park on the road; the music gets louder; the apple tree dies; and the cat gets thinner and thinner. None of these were the outcomes you sought.

What if you had paused first and thought: 'What is the outcome I want?' If so, your inner dialogue could have gone like this:

- -

The outcome I want is for him to listen to my concerns, be reasonable and amend his behaviour. What is the best way

I can achieve this? Can I invite him round for a cup of tea and appeal to his better nature? Could I explain the impact his behaviour is having on me, ask him to compromise, and even ask how I could help him in return?

WHAT! I hate the b*****d – I can't be nice to him. He's the one behaving badly. I am *not* going to reward it.

Well, what's the alternative?

Put my foot down and threaten to call environmental health or the police or get my rugby-playing friends to call round.

Is he the sort that will respond in the way you want to threats like that?

No, but it will make me feel sooo much better!

Is it worth swallowing some pride to have a better chance to get the outcome you want?

Hmmmm – maybe it's worth a try, but it'll take a massive effort to stay calm …

OK. Imagine you're calm. You're going to smile and not raise your voice. Imagine that he also wants things to be better between you. Put yourself in his shoes – perhaps he was justified in cutting back the tree. Listen to what he has to say. He might not really have meant to upset you. Act as if that is true for this meeting.

The type of self-coaching can help you get better outcomes when things go wrong. Get in the habit of this type of thinking and you will start responding very differently to events.

Figure 6.2 shows that creating a gap between the event and our reaction to it gives us a chance to think on purpose and create different meanings from situations. Practising this ability will mean that our reactions to events become more measured and considered, which in turn means we become more flexible, better negotiators and less angry! Even more importantly, we will get more successful outcomes and be happier as a result.

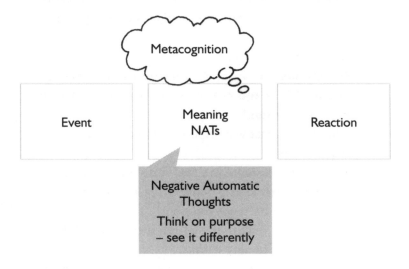

Figure 6.2: Reacting to events.

I'm sorry, I'll think that again

Here are some case studies to illustrate how alternative outcomes can be achieved by thinking in different ways. Changing your thinking changes how you feel, and helps you react differently in stressful situations.

'It's so unfair' – Jez's story

Jez is a team leader who is struggling to find out how to get the best from the more difficult members of his team.

Jez has a new worker in his team. He has put in long hours, working really hard to support her, even though she has often been late, rude and unable to take constructive criticism. One day he finds that she has seen his line manager and has unjustly accused Jez of bullying. Angry and without thinking, Jez decides to tell his line manager just what he feels about this unfounded accusation. His line manager responds by talking about taking statements and starting an internal investigation. Jez loses his temper and finds himself swearing and storming out of the meeting.

Afterwards, Jez not only felt furious with his line manager and his accuser, but also with himself for losing his temper. He returned to his desk feeling a massive sense of injustice, and responds by brooding, generating even more negative instinctive thoughts (see Table 6.2). He acted on them by deciding to sulk and not speak to either his accuser or line manager for the rest of the week.

Jez acted instinctively. He lost his temper, demonstrating an aggression not seen before – and to the wrong person (his line manager). He didn't take the time to assemble evidence to help him explain the support he had given. He didn't realise in time that this accusation would have to be investigated - no matter how misguided it was. He failed to see it from his manager's point of view.

As a result of reacting to his first instinctive thought (see Table 6.2), Jez is now sitting at his desk sulking and feeling victimised. He is having even more negative thoughts which, in his present state of mind, all seem reasonable. There is only one way in which this thinking will take him – especially if his manager has to investigate the allegation without Jez's cooperation and input.

What might have happened if, instead, Jez had deliberately reframed his thinking both before and after his meeting with the line manager?

As soon as he heard the allegation, a good start would have been for him to sit down and ask, 'What outcomes do I want?' He might have thought:

- I want my line manager to appreciate how hard I've tried to support the new worker, and how this shows my leadership potential.
- I want the new worker to take my good advice, act on it and improve her performance.
- I want this accusation to be dropped immediately because it is unfounded.

Bearing these outcomes in mind, he could have examined his first and subsequent instinctive thoughts and reframed them to help him achieve the outcomes he wanted, as shown in Table 6.2.

Table 6.2: Reframing Jez's instinctive thoughts.

Instinctive negative thoughts	WIOIW	Deliberate reframe
How dare she accuse me when I have helped her so much?	I want her to know how I have tried to help.	I wonder if she knows how hard I have tried to help?
My manager believes her rather than me.	I want my manager to see the whole story.	He has to listen to her complaints – it's part of his job.
This is so unfair, and typical of my luck.	I want to be lucky and effective in my job.	Sometimes things don't work as you expect. This is the first time this has happened. What can I learn from it? I need to act in a professional way.

Instinctive negative thoughts	WIOIW	Deliberate reframe
Nothing I say can make a difference now.	I want to learn from this and make a good impression on my manager.	I need to keep calm and make sure I present my manager with evidence of the support I've given the new worker. I need to continue to show her that my attitude is supportive, even during the investigation.

Slow down and think WIOIW (What Is the Outcome I Want – pronounced like a cat's meow!). You can use this mantra in stressful situations, and also in everyday interactions. Think of it as a powerful magnet pulling your emotions down, encouraging slow, deep breathing and a calm, rational state which helps you to make better choices.

Luckily Jez calmed down and phoned a friend who asked him that key question, 'What do you want to happen next?' Jez realised he loved his job and wanted to apologise to his line manager and create a clear plan to move forward and develop his leadership skills. This would mean trying to understand the situation, and even considering why this employee had felt she was being bullied. Sometimes, no matter how unfair it seems, the best approach is to put yourself in someone else's shoes. Jez remembered a mantra from one of his training sessions ('The meaning of your communication is the response you get') and realised he had to take some responsibility for what had gone wrong.

'She's spoiling everything' – Paula's story

Being a parent is one of the hardest challenges of all, and all parents make mistakes.

Paula's daughter Greta was a smart, high-achieving girl with lots to celebrate. It was her sixteenth birthday, and she had been given money to go out shopping and spend on herself before the big family party planned for that evening.

Greta returned from her shopping expedition with bags containing new clothes for the party. She was eager to show them off to her mum. Excitedly she changed into them and with a flourish paraded them for her, saying that she had another surprise for her later. The clothes were bright to the point of fluorescent and, Paula thought, inappropriately revealing. But as Greta was obviously so pleased with them, Paula gritted her teeth and smiled. She smiled, that is, until Greta proudly revealed her surprise – a tongue stud. Her freshly pierced tongue was still swollen, but Greta reassured her mother that it would quickly heal and leave a fabulous silver ball, hardly noticeable to anyone.

Paula was initially shocked into silence. Greta sensed that she had made a mistake but was not about to back down. She said how much she liked it and how many of her friends had one. Paula couldn't conceal her dislike for the stud. She had had no idea this had been her daughter's plan, and absolutely no idea why anyone would want a metal stud in their tongue. Surely, thought Paula, it would damage Greta's teeth, cause infections and give completely the wrong impression if anyone ever spotted it. All these thoughts boiled up and Paula let herself say what she thought about the stud.

The conversation quickly descended into an argument, with mother and daughter screaming at each other. Doors slammed and various items flew through the air, setting the scene for a truly interesting birthday party.

What were the outcomes that Paula wanted?

- To make Greta aware of the possible consequences of her actions.
- To try to get Greta to discuss her plans with her in future.
- To make sure that the birthday party went well despite the surprise.
- To prevent further nasty surprises.

Because of the shock she felt at the moment of the tongue stud reveal, Paula needed to realise that this was the moment when she needed to have massive self-regulation. She needed to think on purpose, curb her instinctive emotional reaction, and consider WIOIW (What Is the Outcome I Want?).

She could have taken a deep breath and said calmly, 'Well, I wasn't expecting that – did it hurt?' 'Why did you decide to have it done?' 'Did you know it can cause the enamel in your teeth to wear away? Let's keep an eye on that, shall we?' 'Let's see what else you've got to wear tonight for the party.'

In the end it was Paula who felt embarrassed that she had lost her temper and made a scene. She swallowed her pride and apologised to her daughter for reacting in such an emotional way, but explained why she had done so. They talked for a long time about how they could make sure a similar situation wouldn't happen again … and hugged. Table 6.3 shows Paula's thought process.

Table 6.3: Reframing Paula's instinctive thoughts.

Instinctive thoughts	Deliberate reframe
What the hell does she think she's done? Why didn't she ask my advice?	She is growing up and becoming more independent.
I just won't have it – I'm still her mother.	I may not be able to control everything now she is growing up.
It's a reflection on my parenting.	It shows she is her own person and not dependent on my approval.
It's gross and embarrassing for me.	Everyone makes mistakes and at least this one can be reversed, eventually.
She has ruined the day.	She thinks she has done something to make her special birthday more exciting and establish her independence.

It's not only your temper you can control by thinking on purpose. Fear can literally paralyse you. Unfortunately, the more you allow your fearful thoughts to guide your actions, the more they will bully you into compliance. Trying to avoid the things you fear makes them grow in importance, feeding them so they grow even stronger. Sometimes they may spread and you may become afraid of other, unrelated things. As I said in Chapter 4, I was terrified of public speaking so I deliberately avoided any situation in which I had to do it. I soon found that I was becoming afraid of speaking in social situations, then speaking on the telephone, then of driving at night. My comfort zone began to shrink, and so did my enjoyment of life. My days were becoming ruined by the ever-present fearful thoughts lurking on the edge of my conscious mind.

Changing my thinking has made me afraid of nothing, because I know now that fear is simply a thought: a thought that I can deliberately reframe. Don't let your thoughts bully you. Challenge them and consider the outcome you really want. It is hard work to change those limiting beliefs – but really worth it. You will grow.

Gary's story

Gary was scared of driving. He had been involved in an accident some years ago when he had skidded and the car rolled over, temporarily trapping him. Ever since, the thought of getting behind the wheel had terrified him. He had tried to drive again and even had some refresher lessons, but somehow he never got round to taking the car out again regularly. He always managed to get lifts, trains or buses to work, and his wife was happy to do the driving for the family. When it came to having a drink at parties, it came in quite handy that he didn't drive!

Then came a time when Gary knew that his wife was going away with friends and his kids would need a lift to judo. At times like this, he wished he could just get in the car and drive, as he had done without a thought for years. So one evening when everyone was busy, he took the keys and went out to the car on the drive.

Even opening the driver's door made his stomach turn. As he sat running his fingers over the steering wheel and trying out the pedals, he felt hot and clammy. Bracing himself, he put the keys in the ignition and started the engine. Glancing in the mirror, he caught sight of his pale, strained face. 'I can't, I just can't,' he thought and reluctantly got out of the car, locking it behind him.

Cursing his weakness, he phoned a friend and asked him to take his children to judo.

What are the outcomes Gary wants?

- To have the freedom to drive his family around.
- Not to have to rely on public transport every day.
- To drive without anxiety.
- To re-establish his pride.

Gary has done some driving since, but his thinking is it is a 'work in progress'. He still finds it anxiety-provoking and tends to avoid it if possible. He will need to drive every day to really reframe the way he sees his driving skills. See Table 6.4 for his thoughts, and how he could reframe them.

Table 6.4: Reframing Gary's instinctive thoughts.

Instinctive thoughts	Deliberate reframe
Sitting in the driver's seat makes me feel so shaky that I won't be able to control the car.	I can remember lots of times I sat here confidently and enjoyed driving.
I won't remember how to change gear, and I may panic when I'm driving.	I am a good, safe driver and it will all naturally come back to me.
I may have an accident and kill someone.	This is highly unlikely. I will actually drive safely and confidently.

Instinctive thoughts	Deliberate reframe
I don't really need to drive – so why put myself through it?	I am reprogramming my thinking so that I can be independent and drive myself around. When I have done it, I will feel proud.

Acting as if …

It can be hard to reframe negative thoughts and thereby take control of your thinking. Your inner dialogue can be really strong as the neural pathways responsible for it may have been set up a long time ago and been strengthened over the years by constant use. Sometimes you have to do more than think differently; you have to act differently – deliberately.

Sometimes you have to fake it. This will be hard and make you feel quite uncomfortable for a while because you will be incongruent, it won't feel real or natural. You will have to pretend to think differently at first. Faking it, however, can have a remarkable impact on the outcome you are seeking, and also on your own thinking and brain chemistry. I speak from experience as an ex-head teacher with responsibility for a multi-million pound budget, 1,500 teenagers and well over 100 staff.

When you're a head teacher, every day can be an adventure – or a terrifying obstacle course. Students could slide down banisters, fall off and crack their skulls. An army helicopter could crash-land on your school field, or a disabled child could be trapped in a lift and then the fire alarm goes off. There could be a financial meltdown and an unannounced visit from an Ofsted inspection team. Staff and children could come to you with terrible personal problems.

All these, and more, happened to me within a year of getting the job. Remaining calm and leading the whole school community through the turbulence was an absolute priority. I am not known for my calm approach in a crisis – 'headless chicken' might best describe my default style in emergencies. However, when I really had to, because I firmly believed it was my job to reassure the children and staff, I could radiate calm confidence and clarity. I could slow down my pace, my thinking, my breathing, and say to myself, 'I can cope with an infinite amount of stress,' over and over again. To this day I can act as if I am completely in control of my emotions and not allow panic to bubble up and disempower me. It is very, very good practice to deliberately *act as if,* it is the ultimate 'thinking on purpose' and it can actually sometimes change your attitude, in my own experience.

Rashid's story

Acting as if ...

Rashid had had a successful year. He had won various bids for work, seen them through and brought in good results for his company. Each project he was involved with was different, and this latest bid had kicked off immediately after he had returned from a wonderful walking holiday in the Alps. But Rashid was not refreshed by the holiday – he still felt tired. Getting to know a new team and putting together another bid had lost its excitement. He found himself feeling stuck in the office, having to bash out figures on a computer and work with other men in suits late into the evening. He found himself getting irritable with his team and, when he finally got home, usually after 9pm, he snapped at his family.

He began to resent his boss' obsession with trivial legal matters, the detailed analysis of figures that were blocking the progress of the bid, and the difficult client. He was sick of dealing with corporate bullshit and smart-mouthed egotists in suits, who simultaneously scared and sickened him. Each day it got worse, he didn't know how much more he could take before he imploded. Frankly, the whole project seemed to be a complete waste of energy, he thought. Time seemed to drag by, and he was stuck in an airless office, chained to a computer all day, then all he had to look forward to was the Tube journey home, going to bed, and it all beginning again tomorrow. He had started waking up with dread lurking in his chest, and he prepared himself for the misery of each new day with strong coffee and the occasional beta-blocker. He desperately wanted to walk out – but with his kids at university and a mortgage, that wasn't possible. There had to be another way.

What are the outcomes Rashid wants?

- To get up in the morning without feeling a sickening dread at the thought of going to work.
- To work with other people and accept their strengths and weaknesses without judging them.
- To do good job and make a difference.
- To feel that what he is doing is worthwhile.

Table 6.5 shows his thoughts – and how they could be reframed.

Table 6.5: Reframing Rashid's instinctive thoughts.

Instinctive thoughts	Deliberate reframe
Another day at the grindstone with people I loathe.	I am going to smile and chill today, so if anyone is grumpy I will recognise their input and ask how I can help improve things.
This corporate bullshit is really grinding me down.	My company has to make a profit and I can see that I am helping with that. I am so lucky to have such a well-paid job that allows me to have fabulous holidays.
The journey to work on the Tube, stuck under someone's armpit, is unbearable.	I am going to think of lovely things or sing a song in my head while under the armpit!
This project is a waste of my time.	I am going to make this project successful and learn everything I can from it.

Putting this type of reframing into practice took an extreme version of 'thinking on purpose'. Rashid really had to 'fake it'. Here is a bit more detail about how he did it.

Rashid decided to think differently. He decided to 'act as if' he loved the project. He could do this by remembering other projects he had enjoyed and felt motivated by. He told himself this project had its good points – there was a fair chance the bid would be successful, and it would be a real money-spinner for his company and so earn him lots of brownie points. He was also learning a lot about legal matters he hadn't come across before. He faked a little smile as he thought to himself that he was really looking forward to his day! He went on to think about what he needed to do next, and decided he would call a team meeting to get some 360-degree feedback. He wanted to find out how others were feeling about the project, and get an idea about whether he was doing a better job than he felt he was.

On the train to work he hummed away and gave up his seat with a smile to a grumpy-looking old lady who seemed to look grateful. He made a determined effort to walk with pace and energy to his office, appreciating the thin sunshine of the autumn morning. When a cyclist nearly ran him down, he waved a cheery, forgiving gesture, and as he walked in the building he said a loud, 'Good morning!' to the busy receptionist. She looked surprised and pleased.

At the team meeting Rashid got valuable positive feedback about how he was doing. The team felt progress was being made and were pleased with how he made them laugh with his satirical comments. He felt quite encouraged to find that the team members were equally frustrated by the obstacles in the path, and the mountain of work there was to do.

Later that day Rashid had a patronising, critical call from the company accountant about team expenses. Normally this would have really irritated him but, thinking on purpose, he reflected on how the accountant's tone was just an expression of his own unhappiness and Rashid decided to feel sorry for him. It felt good to be able to wrest back control over his emotions. Maybe he could get used to 'faking it' – at least until this project was completed.

The project won the business, and the company were pleased with Rashid's work and responded positively to his request to work on a different type of project in future.

Take your mind to a different place

Getting in the habit of surviving tough situations demands the ability to stand back and manage your thinking through metacognition. This can be a powerful protective shield as well as an enabler. Survivors of abuse or solitary confinement talk of being able to take their minds to a different place in order to cope with what they are experiencing. This is the ultimate in managing your thinking. In our everyday world we are often not even conscious that we mentally rehearse every situation before it even happens, often with a natural negative bias.

Managing your mental rehearsals

You are about to make a presentation to colleagues at work, have a job interview or a first date. Days before it happens, you are rehearsing the scene in your mind. Several times over you picture yourself there, hear the words spoken, and feel the anticipated feelings, probably in a number of different ways. Your natural negative bias seeks out and imagines the worst-case scenarios, making you dread them and think they will inevitably happen. Your reptilian brain reacts to these imagined threats, mistakes, embarrassments and disasters so that simply the thought of the impending event gives you sleepless nights and a queasy stomach.

As far as your brain is concerned, the event has actually happened and it went horribly wrong.

Your brain can't differentiate between what you imagine and what actually happens, so all that negatively biased mental rehearsal has just confirmed your worst nightmares. Then your brilliant brain connectors get to work. Remember that the brain looks for patterns to connect to create meaning. When you arrive at that scene you pictured – the conference or interview room, the restaurant for your date – your brain remembers your mental rehearsal. It refers to the beliefs you have already created in your imagination – that this is: (a) a threat and (b) going to go horribly wrong. These beliefs now cause the reptilian brain to react to protect you and – hey presto – you are now in full 'fight or flight' mode with your heart racing, blood pumping, breathing shallow and mouth dry. These symptoms are not useful for performing at your best.

Being able to manage your mental rehearsals helps your brain connect with the outcome you want and make *that* into a self-fulfilling prophecy. This goes beyond the normal thinking on purpose and the WIOIW pause moment and into a much more detailed process of visualising success.

Visualising success

This takes considerable self-discipline, but learning how to habitually stand back and deliberately imagine that events in your life will have a positive outcome will help make you more successful and happier. Visualising success means taking the time to reflect on and recognise your automatic, probably pessimistic, thoughts and, instead, create a detailed picture of the sights, sounds and feelings you actually *want* to have. This means you need to visualise clearly and in detail *exactly* the outcomes you want.

For example, your interview is next week.*

As I walk in for the interview I want to see myself looking

smart, attractive and professional with a confident, pleasant smile. I will be well prepared and when I answer questions I will give lots of detail, speaking fluently and convincingly about my past experience and its relevance to the job. I will feel calm and in control as I make my presentation to the panel. They will be nodding with approval and admiration as I form a rapport with them. There will be a light-hearted atmosphere and I will become aware that they are very keen to recruit me for this post.

Think through the interview moment by moment and visualise yourself seeing, hearing and feeling it as a positive experience. Rehearse the interview going like this over and over again. Doing so will programme your brain to expect a good experience. The more extreme the positive feelings in this mental rehearsal, the more your emotional brain will respond. You need to make your mental rehearsals visualisations of outstanding success, not just mediocre survivals. This may go against your natural modesty – but it works.

As you are preparing your materials for the interview, keep repeating this visualisation as many times as you can so that it starts to feel natural. Sports psychologists use this type of positive visualisation so sportspeople can rehearse getting the perfect bullseye, snooker pot or penalty kick. If you visualise an outstanding performance over and over again, it seeps into your unconscious mind, helping to overcome tension and nerves.

Beware! It is hard not to let doubts creep in and undermine you. Your inner critic might say mockingly, 'Oh, this is stupid. It's all bound to go wrong.' Thoughts like this will be linked to negative visual images and feelings that will threaten all your hard work. Look at them dispassionately and dismiss them for what they are – barriers to growth. Whatever your forthcoming challenge, visualise it going well.

Make it big and bold and an outstanding success in your imagination. Repeat it. And repeat it again.

Once you have felt this work, try to trigger positive mental rehearsals for other aspects of your life, such as when you are facing tough times at work or in family situations. A helpful trick is to use the 'nudge' strategy to help you do this. The nudge strategy was outlined by Thaler and Sunstein in their book of the same title, and shows how the choices we make are swayed by minor, apparently trivial influences. As they said: 'Small and apparently insignificant details can have major impacts on people's behaviour.'[9]

We see this in the placement of supermarket offers on sweet treats, health warnings on cigarette packets, hand sterilisers by the doors of hospital wards. Simple reminders to do the right thing are around us all the time. They nudge people into making certain choices by prompting their brain with temptation: sometimes for commercial reasons, sometimes for the common good. As we move through life in automatic mode, a small nudge can change our behaviour. Supermarkets know this and nudge us to choose more products by putting them in our eye line and reminding our emotional brain that we like them. Even if we have a shopping list we can be unconsciously persuaded to add random, impulse purchases of products that we didn't know we needed.

We can use the nudge technique to snap us out of automatic pilot and help remind us to do our visualisations and repeated rehearsals. Nudge strategies you can use to do this include:

- Making a list and working your way through it.
- Creating a mantra such as 'Think you can' and putting it above your bathroom mirror.

---

9   R.H. Thaler and C.R. Sunstein, *Nudge: Improving decisions about health, wealth and happiness* (London: Penguin, 2009), p. 3.

- Choosing a theme tune such as 'Happy' to hum when negative thoughts creep in.
- Using a physical movement such as deep breathing or shoulder rolls to create states of relaxation.
- Creating a definite physical anchor (an anchor is a shortcut to a state of mind) such as pressing your middle finger and thumb together as you imagine in technicolour the great outcome you want from a situation. This physical act can remind your brain how to feel positive just when you need it.
- Using gentle phone alarms to remind you to check your thinking in stressful situations.
- Writing a symbol or message on your hand, such as a smiley face, to act as a trigger for good thinking.
- Use the mood monitor that came free with this book to nudge yourself into a different mood.

Counter your cynicism

Your internal cynic may be making you feel slightly sceptical and dismissive of visualisation, acting as if, thinking on purpose and the rest. You might think it simplistic that a nudge such as those above can really change the way you think. You could be thinking, 'Who's kidding who?'

That's fine, but the alternative is to roll along on automatic pilot, doing what comes 'naturally' – making decisions that Thaler and Sunstein call 'mindless', unconsciously giving in to temptations that our thinking brain knows are unwise. For example, grazing on that huge bowl of crisps, buying a pair of shoes that look great but don't fit, eating that extra portion, buying that gadget you don't need, loafing on the sofa when you had intended to do 10,000 steps a day.

Since I have been working for myself, I have made a list of tasks to complete each day and I work through them. If I didn't, I would be indulging instead in endless mindless displacement activities like checking emails or Facebook, making unnecessary phone calls to friends, tidying my desk, watching daytime soaps, feeding the fish, etc. etc.

In my kitchen I have a tall mirrored fridge-freezer. It's unusual. It is also a powerful mood enhancer because every time I walk past it (many times a day) I see myself. It has a wonderful effect – it distorts my shape to make me look taller and slimmer than I really am. Even though I know it is a lie, I love it, because in my everyday world I like to see myself like that. For people with anorexia, a life-threatening eating disorder, their own minds distort the image they see in the mirror in the opposite way.

The way we read the world and reflect on it is very powerful. Nudge your reading of the world to make it better for you.

Think your way towards your goals

The following verse is written on a card on my desk. My daughter bought it for me, and it reminds me to appreciate what I have right now:

Be happy for this moment. This moment is your life.

Sometimes we can set our goals for the year and make a list of promises to ourselves of the bad habits we will give up and the courageous decisions we will make. Then another year goes by and we find we haven't quite managed to reach our goals. Goal-setting is so important because it makes us imagine for a brief moment how we could change things, but unless we deliberately think in new ways about those challenges, change probably won't happen. Make sure you spend some time really envisaging your dream goal and thinking about how it would change your life. Then just do it. When you are on your deathbed you won't wish you had procrastinated a little more often during your lifetime! Instead, you may wish you had enjoyed every moment and taken every opportunity available.

Scientists say that there may be an infinite number of parallel universes out there, where different versions of you exist. If you are happy with your relationships, your job, yourself and the way your life is going here and now – enjoy!

If not, try thinking differently and see how you can grow.

Reflect and review

- Our reactions are often instinctive, automatic, 'fast' and based on intuition.
- Intuition is an unconscious process so we can react quickly and we don't have to think about everything. For example, a car comes towards us and we move.
- Some of our fixed mindset ideas are rooted in our unconscious 'fast' thinking, and thereby create attitudes and beliefs.
- Metacognition, or thinking on purpose, can slow down your instinctive reactions and help you check that they are right and helpful.
- Inner dialogue is our link between just reacting and thinking on purpose.
- 'Acting as if' can make us feel different and can help us survive stressful situations and change our attitudes.
- You can use mental rehearsals to take more control of your thinking and ensure the outcomes you want.
- Set goals and targets, but think on purpose as if you *will* achieve them.

Points of view

Q I have always read self-development books and tried to put some of what I have read into practice, but I feel very stuck at the moment. I have been with my partner for ten years and we seem to have lost touch with each other. I've been busy at work and he travels away in his sales job quite often. We don't have children, but love our two dogs – although it's mainly me that walks them and spends time with them.

I have some really good friends and neighbours and now find I prefer spending time with them, even when my partner is around. We seem to have stopped communicating and haven't had sex for months. I have tried having 'date' nights and talking about things, but he shuts down as soon as the conversation gets on to 'us'. I feel exhausted by trying to find solutions, and don't know if I can be bothered any more. I still think the loving, kind man I first fell in love with is in there somewhere, but I can't reach him. I would pack my bags and leave, but we own a house together so it's complicated. My life is so dull and I feel that I am waiting for something to happen … but it never does. Nothing in any self-development book can help me because it isn't something I can change. Help!

A I agree that sometimes books aren't the answer, but the fact that you are interested in self-development raises some questions that may be helpful to consider. What makes you want to read such books? Have you changed since you met your partner? What did you used to like about him? What do you want *exactly* from him? Couples counselling with Relate asks these questions of both of you, so you could ask your partner if he would consider counselling with you.

In the meantime, consider changing the way you communicate. Try thinking, on purpose, as if he is your absolute priority – above friends, dogs, job, and so on, and see how your communication changes. When talking about him, celebrate his good points instead of moaning about his failings. It will take effort and time, but this way you may break the ice between you and be able to explore the possibility of reviving the good relationship you had. Try deciding you still love him and acting and thinking as if you do. Think 'love is a verb': I need to actually do it to feel it.

See what happens. There may be other issues around your lifestyle choices to investigate too. Isn't it always possible to change your house, job, goals … and thinking? Being able to stand back and reflect (exercise metacognition) and think in new ways could help you move your life forward.

Q Every year I make New Year's resolutions to stop drinking and smoking to improve my health. I go on a diet that lasts a few days, sign up at the gym (which lasts a couple of months), but then I find that by February I am back in my old habits. I just can't seem to change – and sometimes I don't even care. What can I do?

A The solution is contained in your last comment. Nothing can change unless you really believe you want to change, that you can change, and that the change will be worth it. Getting fit means having an exercise schedule and being willing to change your eating habits. Make this become *who* you are, not just what you do.

Try a new way of exercising and then thinking about it differently: for example, 'I love my cycle ride into work every day.' Take two days every week to eat much less than normal. Act as if you are enjoying your 'fast' days. Imagine yourself as a non-smoker, fresh-smelling and not a slave to nicotine. Think of yourself as someone who is fit and healthy – and proud of it. Decide first whether you really want to change, start thinking differently, then take action.

Chapter 7

Growing others

The ultimate interpersonal communication skills

This chapter will focus on how to grow others you care about, such as friends and family, using coaching skills to help them manage their thinking. Through growing others in this way, you will also learn to grow yourself. Growing others is a win-win. It is a key skill for the workplace too. To be able to support colleagues to develop a growth mindset will make you a desirable team member or team leader.

The most powerful way to learn something is to teach it to someone else. When you have to connect your ideas together to explain how something works, you deepen your own learning. This is why growing others by sharing what you know about thinking on purpose will make you an expert. However, an even more powerful tool to help your personal growth is to coach others to develop their ability to think differently, to think on purpose and to identify and challenge any fixed mindsets or prejudices they may have.

Coaching is learning how to ask the right questions that tweak other people's thinking.

Being a great coach means helping others find their *own* way towards change and improvement, to help them think on purpose and grow a learning mindset. Good coaches do this in such a way that the person they're helping hardly realises that they are being helped. Coaching skills are also useful for growing your own and someone else's cognitive flexibility – the ability to reflect on your thoughts and decide if you need to think in a different way to get a different outcome.

What happens when friends and family are unhappy and you try to help? Do they ignore your advice and go on to make the same mistakes again and again? It can be very frustrating trying to help people who seem determined to be a victim. Karpman's drama triangle (Figure 7.1) gives us some insight into why, when we try to help other people, it can go badly wrong and we can end up feeling angry.[1]

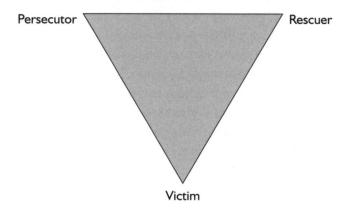

Persecutor   Rescuer

Victim

Figure 7.1: Karpman's drama triangle.

The triangle could go like this: a friend needs help as he feels he is stuck in a dead-end job and is always broke. The strain is destroying his family's happiness. As the 'victim' of these circumstances, he seeks out your help. You want to 'rescue' him by giving him some excellent

---

1   S. Karpman, Fairy tales and script drama analysis, *Transactional Analysis Bulletin* (1968), 7(26): 39–43.

advice. The advice you offer about updating his CV, joining LinkedIn and going on a personal development course is accepted, but is not acted on, and so nothing changes. Several weeks later, you ask your friend about his progress and find out that he is still playing the victim. 'I just haven't had time to do it and it probably wouldn't work anyway,' is his despondent response to your enquiry. Your rescue has failed, so you get annoyed with him and say, 'If you can't be bothered to make some changes then it won't get any better.' You start gently like this, but his continued excuses for inaction make you more and more frustrated and agitated – and you let it show. You've now become the persecutor in your friend's eyes. Initially this will push him further into victim mode but eventually he might hit back, telling you to stop interfering, taking on the persecutor role himself. You then feel hurt and may slip into victim mode, saying plaintively that you were only trying to help.

If we don't stand back and reflect on the outcomes created by our actions, we can find ourselves revolving through these roles during our interactions – experience the associated negative feelings – and still not make any progress towards solving the original issues.

This is often how we deal with our children as they grow up. We want to help them, so we give them a long list of advice and guidance that we know will work for them, as it has worked for us. We want to rescue them because we care for them and we know what is best. When they ignore our advice and continue to swear, stay up late, smoke, take drugs, and reap the consequences, we turn into the persecutor, saying, 'I told you so' and dish out punishments such as grounding them.

They first feel victimised, then angry, and then turn into our persecutor, accusing us of not understanding them, being unfair and being the worst parents in the world. Later, when tempers have cooled, we turn back into rescuers, take up a plate of food to their closed bedroom door, and so it goes.

Think for a moment about your own relationships with family, friends or colleagues and decide where you tend to be situated on the drama triangle. Are you mainly a rescuer, victim or persecutor? Next time, change your role to see what happens.

Consider these two responses to a friend's confession that her partner is emotionally abusing her:

1 You poor thing … You need to dump him.
2 Have you thought about how you would like to be treated by your partner?

Response 2 may seem less sympathetic but might help her think slightly differently and won't reinforce her low self-esteem. Imagining for a moment how things could be different can offer an alternative to the 'victim' identity.

If we can become aware of what we say and how it can come across to the other person, it gives us the opportunity to help others we care about become more resilient and confident. The way we communicate nurtures beliefs and habits in the people around us without us, or them, even realising it.

What is coaching, and why is it so powerful?

One way to avoid the drama triangle described above is to use a coaching method instead of simply trying to 'rescue' people by giving suggestions and solutions to their problems. Fine-tune your advice by turning it into coaching questions. This restores the initiative to the person you're helping and is far less judgemental. It also begins to prompt mental rehearsals of solutions in the head of the person you are talking to and, as we discovered earlier, this can create powerful self-fulfilling prophecies.

Whether you are trying to lead your team or help a friend, developing a coaching style will deliver better long-term results. Being a good coach will also help you develop your own empathy skills.

Coaching is about helping someone move their thinking forward and find new solutions through asking powerful questions. It naturally develops a growth mindset because it challenges people to reflect and learn to find new ways to move forward themselves, thereby growing new neural pathways. New neural pathways fashion new habits so that we can change and be flexible in the face of challenges.

A good coach can hold a mirror up to our thoughts and reflect them back for consideration. If you've been mulling over a problem for weeks, you can get stuck or overwhelmed by it. If you ask a coach for help, your coach has the task of allowing you to explore your mind and voice your own solutions. The best conclusion at the end of the coaching process would be for you to say, 'When I thought about it, I realised I had the answer all the time!'

The personal qualities of a coach

Good coaches have a growth mindset and believe that intelligence and capability can be grown through effort and reflection. They can suspend their natural tendency to be judgemental of others and avoid giving direction. In addition, a great coach helps someone:

- recognise their strengths and build their self-esteem
- believe that they have all the answers to any problems within themselves

- move outside their comfort zone
- become curious about how they think
- take personal responsibility and accountability
- set their own goals and identify actions to commit to
- break down big goals into manageable steps.

Great coaches are also:

- authentic and honest
- non-judgemental and non-critical, even when encouraging personal responsibility
- willing to observe, listen and question to raise self-awareness
- motivated to help people grow and are willing to learn from their coaching experience
- able to think that people (and groups of people) are not 'broken' and do not need to be 'fixed', and believe that they have all the resources and strength they need to solve their own problems.

The very best coaches believe in the endless potential of other people. Can you fully accept the following statement?

Everyone has inside them the resources they need to achieve their full potential.

Whenever you are coaching you need to 'act as if' the above is an inescapable truth.

Anyone who is willing to learn through practice can become a coach, but the motivation to become self-aware and the humility required to reserve judgement is essential. Although it seems like an altruistic act to coach others, the practice of using questions to help others find new ways to grow is also one of the most satisfying ways to grow yourself.

Who do you think is in control?

When something doesn't go to plan, it's easy to blame something or someone else: 'You don't understand me', 'The database is down', 'My manager is useless', 'The admin staff are off sick', 'The market has taken a downturn', 'My dog has just died', 'I don't have the time', etc.

This is taking what's known as an *external* locus of control. The belief here is that we can do nothing to change the current situation because of something happening outside of ourselves, which is therefore out of our control. A classic fixed mindset attitude!

Alternatively, when we have an *internal* locus of control we are more likely to believe that we are responsible for what is happening in our life and work.

Successful people tend to have an internal locus of control. Take these examples:

- 'I have an opportunity to really improve delegate numbers.'
- 'Perhaps I could design this better.'
- 'Do I need to say it differently?'
- 'What can I learn from that?'
- 'Maybe I need to think again about my strategy.'
- 'I could try my own ideas to help the sales team be more efficient.'
- Or even 'I could be wrong.'

Having an internal locus of control simply means that you take some responsibility and that if you want things to change, you are willing to change yourself. People who believe that what happens to them is out of their control tend to moan a lot about things, but rarely reflect on what *they* could do about it.

From 'I can't' to 'I can' – a coaching journey through words

Language is powerful. A coach can help tweak the language someone habitually uses and thereby change their mindset and thinking patterns. Coaches use the language of possibility and avoid the language of certainty and absolutes. This helps break through limiting beliefs.

If you are coaching someone, challenge language they might use (such as 'can't', 'never', 'have to', 'must', 'should' or 'ought to'). Encourage instead the language of possibility (see Table 7.1) ('can', 'could', 'maybe', might', 'perhaps', 'possible'). Coaches should encourage people to take a journey from the past to the present, eventually leading to how the future could be.

People being coached often begin the journey with an external locus of control and use limiting language – the language of impossibility. Your job as a coach is to try to change this mindset by employing the language of possibility shown in Table 7.1.

Table 7.1: Different language creates different thought processes.

Language of impossibility	Language of possibility
I can't do …	What if you could?
I ought to …	How could you … ?
I should do …	How about … ?
I have to … /It's compulsory	Why?

Language of impossibility	Language of possibility
I have never …	How could this be an opportunity for you to …?
I am absolutely sure.	Who else could support you in …?
He always makes me feel …	Is there ever a time when you do not feel …?
It's traditional …	How could you use your imagination here?
That is just how it is …	I'm curious – according to whom?
I have never done that/No one has ever done that.	What if you did …?

The language of possibility uses questions that try to develop a habitual internal locus of control in the person being coached. Instead of them finding excuses and someone else to blame, they begin to take more responsibility and thereby take control. If you are helping friends or colleagues cope with challenges, the language of possibility gives you the chance to help them find their own solutions and begin a long-term change in their thinking.

Building a rapport for effective coaching

Really effective coaches know how to build a brilliant rapport with the person they are coaching. If you can build a rapport, you will make an emotional connection with your friend or colleague that will help them commit to moving forward. Rapport is a comfortable, harmonious relationship between two people or a group where everyone understands each other and communicates well. It is easy to see when people have it. When people get on well and feel understood, they are more likely to be prepared to rise to challenges discussed with a coach.

Practise forming a rapport with someone, it will help you in all aspects of your relationships, at work and at home. Try to match and mirror their body posture and eye contact – both are signs of unconscious rapport. To establish rapport you may begin a sentence with the same words or use similar actions, intonation or body language when they are speaking. If you are getting on with someone you might hear them say that they feel they have known you for longer than they actually have, or that you really seem to understand where they're coming from.

Establishing a good rapport and communication can mean the difference between a successful and an unsuccessful meeting with a colleague or friend. If you have a natural rapport, great, but there will be times when the other person is not responsive. The very best coaches coax, adapt and adjust until it works.

Take responsibility for how others see you

Loneliness does not come from having no people about one, but from being unable to communicate the things that seem important to oneself, or from holding certain views which others find inadmissible.

Carl Jung[2]

2   Jung, *Memories, Dreams, Reflections*, p. 356.

'The meaning of your communication is the response you get.' This is a presupposition in neuro-linguistic programming. It means that it is up to you (not the other person) to change your communication style if the response you get isn't what you want. How much do you agree with it?

There is a clear link with the locus of control here. If you want the message you deliver to be received, you must be aware of your delivery, and adjust it when necessary. This means you must be flexible and adaptable, to make others feel comfortable and communicative. You are responsible for making them relax and talk to you, so you must continually adapt your body language, tone, language, volume and pace to suit them, rather than the other way round.

How not to take responsibility for your communication:

'You just seemed irritated and in a hurry.'

'I didn't mean to … I think it was you who was in a bad mood.'

'Everything you say to me sounds patronising and superior.'

'Well, I can assure you I didn't mean it – you must have a complex.'

Instead try:

'That isn't what I meant. Perhaps if I rephrase it like this …'

'I'm so sorry that I came across like that. Let me put it another way …'

Forming a rapport is about understanding how your messages are received. Your body language, expression and tone of voice are hugely important in this. Be adaptable and ready to change your body language if it isn't working.

Listening

When we are genuinely listened to, it can help us to gain a better understanding of our situation and assist us to discover new solutions. Truly listening to someone else's point of view to understand how they think, and are motivated, is a vital skill. Finding out what truly inspires a colleague or friend, or what excites or interests them, is a skill that you can learn. It is about listening not only to what is being said, and how they are saying it, but also listening to what they are *not* saying.

Tips for active listening

1　Be aware of your own prejudices and perceptions.
2　Ask clarifying and open questions.
3　Keep your advice, opinions and assumptions to yourself.
4　Summarise and paraphrase to show you are listening.
5　Listen with your eyes as well as your ears. Be actively interested in what the other person is saying.
6　Use empathy to place yourself in your friend/colleague's shoes. How might they be feeling right now?
7　Spend more time listening than talking: 80%–20%.
8　Keep your full attention on the coachee.
9　Do not dominate the conversation with your own thoughts or ideas.
10　Pay attention – turn off your internal dialogue.
11　Do not complete your coachee's sentences.

12 Plan your response after your coachee has spoken, not while they are speaking.

The skill of questioning

Coaching questions are powerful and need to demonstrate genuine curiosity and show a belief that your friend can find the answers to their issues within themself. The idea is to encourage the other person to think beyond the present problem and search out new ways to see solutions.

To do this, the coach has to ask various questions that encourage self-reflection. The coach does not need to know the answers, but will need to adjust the questions constantly to keep the thinking moving forward.

Questions that encourage ownership

Carefully worded coaching questions can help your friend or colleague realise that they are expected to find their own answers, such as:

- What would you like to focus on today?
- What do you want to achieve?
- Why is that important to you at the moment?
- How can you word that goal more specifically?
- How can you measure that goal?
- How do you want to begin this work?
- Where do you stand now?
- What could be your next step?
- What strategies/ideas do you plan to implement before our next coaching session?

Questions that draw out ideas and information

The purpose of questioning is to acquire new information or to generate new ideas. Neutral questions will help do this:

- What is your perception of ... ?
- How do you feel about ... ?

Open questions increase the chance of getting carefully considered replies:

- What do you want to happen?
- What options do you have?
- What could be your next step?
- When would you like to achieve this?
- When/Where will you do ... ?

Questions that suggest that there is an alternative or a choice also encourage ownership:

- Is this something that you could implement next week, or do you need planning time?
- Do you prefer option A, B or C?

'How' questions can help someone visualise future possibilities and actions:

- How will you ... ?
- How are you going to ... ? (The question presupposes that action will be taken.)
- How are you going to implement this new strategy? (This presumes that the strategy will be implemented.)

Avoid 'why?' questions

'Why?' questions give an opportunity for the person you're working with to make excuses or give long explanations. The idea of coaching is to lead the coachee forward towards a solution – not to go back into history. The 'why?' question can also imply judgement: 'Why did you do that?'

Motivating questions

After listening, asking the right questions at the right time is the best tool you have as a coach. You need to be relentlessly curious about the actions your colleague or friend will take to help them get motivated to take action. For example:

- If this book were to prove to be useful to you, how would you know?
- What would you do differently in the way you grow others?
- What else?
- Who else will know that this book has been of use to you?
- When will they see you doing it?
- Where will you do it?
- What will they hear you saying?
- What else?
- How will you know it worked?

These questions are called 'open' questions and all begin with 'when', 'who', 'how' and 'where'. They are designed to encourage a deeper level of thinking. A 'closed' question, on the other hand (e.g. Is this book useful to you?), will lead to a 'yes' or 'no' answer. Here, deeper thinking is required. Table 7.2 contains examples of different types of question, and suggests when they could be used.

Table 7.2: Different types of coaching question.

Type of question	Example	Use to …
Open (can't be answered 'yes' or 'no')	'What would you like to focus on?' OR 'Tell me something about …'	Get the person you are working with to open up and tell you about their issues. Understand what they are hoping to achieve. Reinforce the belief that the solution is in their hands.
Closed (use for a specific purpose, as they can limit dialogue)	'Did it work?' 'Is that something that you would be willing to do?'	Get a 'yes' or 'no' response.
Clarifying	'What does that mean?' 'Could you be more specific?' 'How would someone else describe this situation?'	Find out the facts. Increase understanding.

Type of question	Example	Use to ...
Reflecting	'What is another way that you could ... ?' 'What would have to change in order for X to happen?'	Reverse a statement or question by rephrasing and sending it back to the person you are working with. Keep them talking.
Hypothetical	'If you had to plan an event tomorrow, what resources would you use?'	Test possible strategies to use in certain situations.
Challenging (these questions may need more time for the coachee to respond)	'What is actually preventing you from ... ?' 'Why do you think this is the case?' 'What gives you the most anxiety here?' 'What is the truth?'	Unblock barriers to progress. Get greater awareness of the problem. Give a different perspective.
Reframing	'You said you haven't seen any improved support in the office, but what would it look like if you did?' 'What would you do if there was no chance of failure?'	Re-examine a belief/ evidence.

Coaching conversations

Here are a couple of examples of conversations that use coaching questions to help someone think in a different way about a problem.

Jenny: I can't seem to do anything without worrying about it endlessly. I'm driving myself mad and it seems to be getting worse. I used to worry about terrorist attacks when I worked in London, but now I get just as worked up if my relatives and their kids are coming for lunch. I used to think nothing of throwing amazing dinner parties before I had my kids.

Eve: What happened the last time you hosted a lunch for them?

Jenny: I had to tidy up the house, get the kids looking nice, prepare salad and pizza. It was all a bit manic. I didn't sleep the night before for thinking about it.

Eve: And how did it turn out?

Jenny: It went well in the end. We all had a lovely time, after I'd calmed down a bit.

Eve: What made it lovely – the food, the tidy house?

Jenny: No. It was the kids playing together and having a lovely catch-up with our family. We all went for a walk together to the local playground.

Eve: What is it exactly that worries you about your relatives visiting?

Jenny: Being ready in time, making sure the house is looking good and the food is nice.

Eve: What is the visit for?

Jenny: It's to get together, catch up on news and see each other's kids, but I don't want them to think my standards have slipped.

Eve: What are your standards?

Jenny: Tidy house, quality refreshments, and perfect kids.

Eve: Do you think those standards matter to your visitors?

Jenny: Some of them may think, 'She's letting it all go' or 'She's not coping.'

Eve: Is that what you think?

Jenny: Sometimes, I do think that, but generally I muddle through.

Eve: Are your children happy?

Jenny: Of course they are. We have our ups and downs, but we have loads of fun and they are enjoying nursery and school. They're lovely kids.

Eve: So you have happy kids and can welcome visitors to your home for an enjoyable lunch. What needs to change here?

Jenny: Nothing, I suppose, apart from my expectations.

Eve: How could you change those?

Jenny: Stop expecting the worst … Maybe focus on what really matters.

Eve: What does really matter?

Jenny: Being happy and relaxed – me *and* the kids.

Eve: How can you achieve that?

Jenny: Take some shortcuts on food – use pre-prepared, etc. Lower my expectations of a tidy house, etc. Don't expect to be the perfect hostess because nobody else expects that of me. It's about the company – the warm welcome I can give.

Eve: Can you see yourself really feeling like that next time?

Jenny: I don't want my standards to slip, though.

Eve: What is the thing you most want to have high standards in now? Housework, hostessing, motherhood?

Jenny: Of course mothering is the most important thing
now ... Maybe I do need to adjust my thinking so I
get my priorities right. Nothing is more important
than the job I do as a mum. I think I need to stop and
think, 'What really matters the most?' from now on.

Here, this type of questioning helps Jenny to reflect on how her thinking may be fine-tuned to prioritise what really matters for her health
and happiness. If you're coaching a friend, relative or work colleague,
the purpose is to reflect back their thinking and help them see that the
solution is in their own hands.

Applying this approach in a work interview

Imagine that a new salesperson in your team started well, but her performance has deteriorated. Look at this coaching approach.

Manager: What have been the highlights of your working
year?

Jo: I managed to sell several sponsorship deals and
met my target for delegate numbers in the first
half of the year.

Manager: What worked well for you to get these successful
outcomes?

Jo: Well ... I was particularly persistent with some
clients, even when they said no first time. I managed to charm them a bit and keep them talking

until in the end they saw sense!

Manager: What are your targets for the coming year?

Jo: My numbers have fallen off badly in the second half, so I need to have a more tactical approach.

Manager: Have you changed your style?

Jo: No, but I think I may have used up all my charm offensive and I need to find other ways. But it's so hard out there, and people don't want to buy. It's the market.

Manager: Has the market changed?

Jo: I suppose so. People don't seem to want to talk any more – they're so busy. That makes me wary about cold-calling.

Manager: Do you think your wariness may be affecting your outcomes? Other sales are doing well.

Jo: Yes, I'm scared I've lost my touch.

Manager: Are you making as many calls as you were?

Jo: No – I sort of dread it. I hear the irritation in people's voices and I feel a sense of rejection. I hate failure and I'd rather not call when I feel like that.

Manager: So what will your new tactical approach to boost your numbers look like?

Jo: I have to rethink my approach and be more positive and uplifting.

Manager: How have you done that in the past?

Jo: I mentally rehearsed the call going well; I kept my tone light and positive; trimmed down the small talk and tried to focus on the benefits for the customer.

Manager: How can you overcome the rejections?

Jo: Move on to the next call quickly, I think. Don't

> dwell on it or take it personally. Just bounce back and crack on playing the numbers game. The more calls I make, the more likely it is that I will have a successful one eventually. It's the nature of the beast.

Manager: How are you going to make sure this happens after today?

Jo: I need a prompt card, maybe saying: 'Bounce back. Crack on. Keep smiling.' You can tell even on the phone if someone is smiling. I used to smile all the time but haven't smiled so much lately. That needs to change.

- -

You can see that in this interview the manager is seeking to build confidence and purposeful thinking to restore Jo's performance when her initial – perhaps naive – enthusiasm has had a reality check.

These examples, from very different situations, show how a coaching approach can help people change their thinking and see the situation in a different way. We could just offer advice and guidance and this may also help. We could sympathise and confirm how impossible things are – which will feel good and be appreciated. Or we can help someone develop the habit of thinking differently, so that changes are more sustainable. As we encourage coachees to think on purpose in different ways, we are giving them a valuable tool for coping with anything that life can throw at them.

Reflect and review

- Helping other people develop and overcome their challenges helps us to learn about ourselves.

- Learning to be a good listener and asking the right questions can help other people change.
- Leadership is the process of growing other people's potential and developing their growth mindset.
- Coaching is the best way to help other people own their own change so that it sticks.
- Coaching is one way to help your colleagues, friends and family think differently.

Points of view

Q Some people can't be coached! Although I agree with the principles of coaching and helping move people forward, some of my colleagues are determined to put up barriers. My job is to coach some of our call-centre staff to improve their customer response. It has worked very well with some of the team, and I have the feedback to prove it. But there is one operator who will not even engage with the process. She is a larger-than-life character and is a bit of a livewire, but feels her telephone style is already perfect. It isn't, because she is slow to pick up and is brusque and argumentative at times. When I try to coach her she looks away, answers in single syllables, and sighs deeply. She sees it as a waste of time and tells everyone else that is what she thinks too! Any ideas?

A Do you think the whole notion of being coached is challenging this lady's self-esteem? You stress that she is an extrovert who has a lively style. Maybe this is the way in for you. If you use the self-disclosure model, you can reveal some of the challenges you have found in your own coaching role – perhaps highlighting some of the mistakes you have made. Try saying, 'I don't always get it right – is there ever a time when you feel like that?'

It also sounds like she needs to focus on developing her empathy. Get to the root of her arguments with customers and find out why she gets angry or offhand with them easily.

Questions like 'What makes you feel good about your job?' or 'What is the best thing you have done this week?' will put her in the right state of mind to think about things she might like to change. Maybe you could train her as a coach and let her try coaching you, so that she can see how to ask the right questions to influence someone else's thinking.

Taking baby steps with this type of challenging coachee will teach you so much about how to help someone to think differently. If you can make progress so that she is actually willing to reflect on her practice, you will have made a real difference.

Chapter 8

Helping our children choose to grow

All parents want the best for their children. The academic demands of school, the use of social media, and navigating their way through friendships means the pressure on our youngsters is higher than ever. This is of great concern to parents and teachers, as they want children to be happy and grow up confident about entering the world of work.

A recent report by the Children's Society (2015) found that English children's self-rating placed them 14th out of 15 countries for life satisfaction, and lowest for self-confidence. The report went on to say that 'The findings indicate that children in England fare particularly poorly in terms of their feelings and perception of themselves and also their feelings about their life at school.'[1]

Our schools have an understandable focus on teaching knowledge to achieve improved examination results, but non-academic factors such as resilience and empathy also have a profound impact on our children's success beyond school. With their happiness and wellbeing at stake, we need young people to grow up being able to think on purpose and so help them avoid becoming victims of mental illness or underachievement.

---

[1] The Children's Society, *The Good Childhood Report 2015*. Available at: www. childrenssociety.org.uk/sites/default/files/TheGoodChildhoodReport2015.pdf, p. 62.

There is a growing body of evidence to suggest that mindset affects diverse outcomes, from academic attainment to psychological wellbeing, from character capabilities to workplace skills.

L. Reynolds and J. Birdwell[2]

The executive summary of the Demos report also found that the development of a 'growth mindset' approach in schools was proving to be a promising solution to the problems children face, saying: 'The evidence presented in this report suggests that mindset development is not just a promising way to improve grades: it is a powerful way to develop healthier, more capable young people ready to meet the challenges of twenty-first-century life.'[3]

This report argues that mindset is as important a predictor of academic achievement as socio-economic background, which suggests that teachers and parents need to apply and share much of the advice in this book with their children. The executive summary finishes by saying: 'Growth mindset can affect a wide range of behaviours, from sense of agency to self-confidence. If these interventions can help us raise academic attainment, tackle social immobility and improve the mental health of young people, then this potential needs to be explored further, with urgency and ambition.'[4]

My own experience as a parent with three children has taught me so much about the challenges we face in nurturing our children's attitudes to life and learning. They all inherit different characteristics and abilities, so helping them to fulfil their potential as happy, healthy citizens is one of the hardest jobs in the world – but also the most

2 L. Reynolds and J. Birdwell, *Mind Over Matter* (Demos, 2015). Available at: www. demos.co.uk/project/mind-over-matter/, p. 10.
3 Reynolds and Birdwell, *Mind Over Matter*, p. 10.
4 Reynolds and Birdwell, *Mind Over Matter*, p. 11.

satisfying. Helping children develop a growth mindset so that they grow up loving to learn, relishing challenge and being confident about handling peer group pressure has to be a priority for parents and carers.

Give your child the growth mindset workout

As a parent you can grow your own mindset at the same time as teaching your children the growth mindset message, by encouraging and embedding the following attitudes and behaviours at home and, crucially, by *modelling* them for your children every day:

- Learning grows your brain. No matter what our starting point, we can always grow our intelligence.
- Intelligence can be learned; effort is the path to mastery.
- Praise and reward effort and strategy, not only outcomes or intelligence. Avoid obsessing over the end result.
- Reflect on learning as a journey that has ups and downs but stress that, above all, we keep moving forward.
- Celebrate the struggle of learning, because that is when your brain is growing.
- Seek out and respond to feedback, particularly constructive criticism.
- Be inspired by other people's success: find out how they did it and what you can learn from it.
- Expand your comfort zone by taking on the challenges you find hard and scary.
- Understand your brain and how it works best, so that you can maximise its potential. That includes understanding anxiety and the power of the reptilian brain state that elicits 'fight or flight' responses (see Chapter 4).

Teaching children how their brains work and how to manage their thinking will help them develop a growth mindset. But it is everyday conversation that impacts the most on their inner dialogue and helps them habitually think about growth, rather than about being judged. Have a look at the checklist below – practise the 'Do says' and watch out for the 'Don't says'.

Growth mindset top tips for parents

Sometimes we don't realise that words which we think encourage and praise can actually undermine our children's ability to become the best learners they can be. All our words and actions are processed by their reptilian and emotional brains for meaning. Are you sending messages that suggest you are judging them, or are you sending them messages that suggest you are supporting them to learn and grow?

To help your child reach their potential and be emotionally resilient try some of the sentences in Table 8.1.

Table 8.1: Giving feedback to develop a growth mindset.

Don't	Don't say	Do	Do say
Praise their intelligence and talents – as if they are fixed.	'You must get 10/10 – it's the only result that matters because you are so bright.'	Praise their effort rather than focus on the outcome.	'I'm so proud of how hard you are trying, and how much you're learning.'

Don't	Don't say	Do	Do say
Judge their outcomes as either good or bad.	'You're so talented – I expected more from you.' Or: 'This is full of mistakes – you can do better!'	Give lots of feedback about what they have done, the strategies they used to do it, and what they could do next – without criticising or judging.	'You have written such an exciting story – how about redrafting and checking some of the spellings I have underlined to make it better still?'
Make them feel that all that matters is their scores and grades.	'You got an A – that's brilliant. You need to keep getting good grades if you're ever going to be successful.'	Focus on what they are learning and strategies which they are developing and celebrate those.	'You have really tried hard with those sums – how did you work them out?'

Don't	Don't say	Do	Do say
Get upset if they can't do it/let them see you are disappointed/ that you think they are useless.	'Are you too stupid to read that book? Anyone your age should be able to do that.'	Help them realise that mistakes are part of learning, and you only learn by making mistakes and sticking at it until you learn new strategies to make progress.	'Did you find that book hard with all those difficult words? Just think how much vocabulary you are learning if you get through it all.'
Demonstrate you are stuck in your ways and nervous about learning new things.	'I don't do foreign languages and I'm no good at maths, so I'd rather not bother.'	Model a growth mindset yourself by sometimes getting it wrong and showing your children how you learn from it.	'I'm finding it really hard to learn a few Spanish phrases for our holiday, but I'm going to stick at it!'

Don't	Don't say	Do	Do say
Praise only when they get it all right.	'You've only done five questions. I thought you could do at least ten.'	Praise them for specific achievements and persistence.	'I'm impressed with how you have found a new way to understand algebra. You stuck at it, tried different ways to do it, and I'm so proud.'
Make judgements about their ability and compare them with other children.	'I hope your teacher doesn't think it's only you who can't do this, because I bet all your friends can.'	Help them fix it when they make a mistake.	'You got it wrong, but that's OK because now you can learn from this and find out how to get it right.'
Let them think you can learn and make progress without the pain of hard work!	'If it's too hard, don't do it – we don't want you to get upset.'	Talk to them about the learning process and journey.	'What have you learned today that has really pushed you out of your comfort zone?'

Don't	Don't say	Do	Do say
Advise them that they don't have to do anything they don't want to do.	'It's not fair if you get it wrong – your teacher should help you more. If you don't like it, you shouldn't have to do it.'	Help them choose challenging tasks that stretch them, even if they may not get everything right.	'Isn't it exciting when you have to work very hard on something and eventually you get it? Well done!'

Other top tips for growing resilient children with a growth mindset are:

- Encourage them to eat different foods, watch different television programmes, make new friends, and expand their comfort zones.
- Debate and discuss the news and world issues, showing tolerance and understanding of a variety of views.
- Teach them to reason and argue their opinion.
- Show them that you are not set in your ways by learning about their world (and not judging it).
- Share stories of your own mistakes and challenges.
- Talk about their day at school like this: 'What did you find hardest today, and how did you stick at it?' instead of, 'What score did you get in that test?'
- Make up stories about children who find things hard and struggle, but learn a lot on the way.
- Encourage them to learn to sing, dance, play a musical instrument, act in school productions, speak in debates, play sports, play computer games, go camping, do part-time jobs, run charity events. The more varied their interests, the more they develop a

growth mindset.

- Be a role model – learn to dance, sing, speak Spanish, or play tennis – anything that involves a struggle!

Try not to tell them they are brilliant or beautiful too much – that can be hard to continually live up to.

Growth mindset schools

Part of my current job involves training teachers to create a growth mindset culture in their classrooms and across the whole school. Schools that use thinking on purpose strategies for growing resilience are creating a powerful lever for school improvement. Indications that your child's school does this include:

- Classroom teaching that celebrates the struggles, processes and strategies inherent in learning.
- Teachers who encourage your child to be a flexible, confident learner, to try out new things, and develop a range of learning strategies when they are stuck.
- The school creates an inclusive atmosphere with zero tolerance of 'put-downs', and encourages children to give unconditional support to others' progress.
- Parents are invited into the classroom to learn with the children and help with projects as often as possible.
- The school shares the latest educational research with parents and welcomes parents to attend sessions on how they can best support their child's learning.
- Teachers and teaching assistants model a growth mindset by being outstanding learners themselves, and share this attitude with their classes.

- There is a valued programme of personal development for all students and teachers, in addition to academic achievement.
- Children (and staff) know how their brains work and how they learn best. The school shares a basic understanding of neuroscience and how to maximise learning with parents and students.
- Assessment includes self-assessment (where children mark their own work) and peer assessment (where children mark each other's work).
- The feedback given to students focuses on effort and progress, helping children take the next steps to learning themselves.
- You should be able to see in their books how your children have responded to the feedback – have they corrected mistakes and improved their work themselves?
- Students are rewarded for their effort as well as their attainment.
- Students are challenged to stretch their own comfort zones academically, physically and personally, to promote resilience, confidence and flexibility.
- Students know what their strengths are and what they need to do to improve.
- There is a full and engaging extracurricular programme that encourages a wide range of interests beyond the usual sports and clubs. School music, drama and dance productions are encouraged for all children.
- The curriculum involves student-led projects, presentations to other children and real-world experiences, in addition to examination courses.
- Communication skills are at the heart of school improvement, with regular communication skills challenges such as public speaking, debating and performance for every child.
- The school website shows that learning is at the heart of its vision and development.

See www.jackiebeere.com for examples of useful teaching resources to develop growth mindset in classrooms.

Three useful questions you can ask a school to discover whether it has a growth mindset at the heart of its culture are:

1   What are your priorities for the children in this school?
2   How do you make sure *all* children fulfil their personal and academic potential here?
3   How can I help my child at home to make the most of their school experience?

Questions you could ask your child at the end of a school day

What did you learn today that surprised you?

Did you make any good mistakes today?

How did you learn from them?

What did you do today that was so hard it made your brain grow?

How did you help someone else learn something new today?

Can you help me choose a recipe for dinner/plants for the garden/a birthday present for your gran (or anything else outside their comfort zone!)?

Growing a growth mindset

What do we want our children to be like at school? What do we want them to do? What do they need to have every day to be like that? Read Tables 8.2 and 8.3, and then think about whether these are relevant to you too.

Do you want your children or yourself to have values like the ones shown in Table 8.2, and follow them? The table also shows what anyone needs to do and have in order to realise these values.

Table 8.2: Realising values.

Be	Do	Have (every day)
Ambitious	Expect more of themselves	Challenges Goals
Resilient	Never give up	Reward for effort Learning strategies
Risk-taking	Try new things	Choice Challenge – the opportunity to fail
Curious	Ask questions	Engaging tasks Connected learning
Flexible	Work in different ways	Creativity Variety
Self-managing	Take feedback well, and use it to improve	Success criteria Targets
Collaborative	Communicate	Pair/group projects Presentations/debates

What other values are important to you or your children? Design your own tables.

Now think about the beliefs needed to underpin these values, and how they can be encouraged in our inner dialogue (Table 8.3).

Table 8.3: Inner dialogues to encourage beliefs.

Belief	Inner dialogue
My brain can grow	'The harder I work, the more intelligent I can get.'
Change is possible	'I know I have always liked doing things that way, but today I'm determined to do it differently.'
Learning is the key	'I want to pass tests, but I know that the strategies and skills I'm learning are the key to my future.'
Helping others helps me	'If someone else gets it right, I want to see what they have done – and what I can learn from them.'
Effort and challenge are essential for learning	'If it is making me feel uncomfortable and frustrated, it is because I am growing new neural pathways.'

Finally, what should we – and our children – do every day to encourage a growth mindset?

- Think on purpose
- Understand how we learn
- Try to learn in many different ways
- Work with different people
- Seek out feedback
- Ask questions
- Learn something new
- Reflect on and review how and what you have learned
- Teach others
- Share ideas and work
- Watch how others learn
- Learn to be a mindset coach
- Practise again and again
- Stick at something
- Set challenging targets
- Push yourself to do the things you find hardest

Parents beware …

Don't overprotect your children. No matter how hard it is for us to think about, our children will have trials ahead of them. They will fall out with friends, find some learning hard, get left out, want to hide from some challenges, get anxious about things, fail some tests, feel sad at times, and have to face all the rest of life's highs and lows.

Experiencing difficulties is essential to prepare them for their future. Vaccinations work by giving our immune system a mild dose of something nasty, so it can recognise and protect us from life-threatening illnesses later on. In the same way, experiencing and surviving the difficulties, frustrations, fears and anxieties of life when young will help your children find strategies to cope with them, and so help them become more resilient later in life. If we try to protect them from everything when they are young, we do not immunise them against the difficulties ahead of them.

Talk to your children about their feelings. Acknowledge them and show them how to think on purpose in ways that make them stronger. This may not completely protect your children from anorexia, self-harm or other serious mental health issues, but it could help them become less emotionally vulnerable as they grow up. Having a fixed mindset, of course, can sometimes be a powerful way to achieve success in sport or music or any specialism. A passion for developing certain knowledge or skills will lead to high standards and the dedication that is required to perform at the highest level. Our job is to help our talented children keep a healthy balance so that if they don't (or even if they do) become an Olympic athlete or famous musician, life is still happy and successful for them.

I hope some of the advice in this book has helped you – it has certainly helped my own children, who have had their fair share of challenges to contend with. Don't try to shield them too much from life as they grow up, because one day they won't have you there to protect them. Our job is to give them the gift of independence and the courage to grow and learn.

Helping other people to grow will definitely help you learn how to grow also. When you practice these strategies on yourself and the people around you, it develops your own thinking. In fact, you'll probably find that you can't help yourself from self-coaching. Sometimes it can even be very irritating to be reminded to push yourself outside your comfort zone. If anyone in our family baulks at a new challenge – whether it be taking part in a charity event, a hike up a mountain, learning a new language or changing jobs – they are reminded to choose to grow. From time to time, everyone needs to be reminded of that message. If we can happily laugh at ourselves when we try new challenges and make mistakes or fail hopelessly, we keep our self-esteem intact and model a growth mindset for our children.

Reflect and review

- Parents and teachers need to nurture a growth mindset in their children for happiness as well as academic success.
- The language you use with your children can help develop resilient or resistant attitudes to learning.
- Your child will learn to cope with the challenges of life with confidence if you support them to push themselves outside their comfort zone.
- You can find out if the school your child attends promotes a growth mindset.
- By helping your child develop a growth mindset for learning, you will learn how to model it yourself.

Points of view

Q My son is a sensitive high-achiever who was reading before he went to school and has always come top in tests throughout primary school. He is quite highly strung, so we have always really encouraged him by building his confidence and telling him how proud we are of his achievements. He gets rewards when he comes top of the class, and we are fighting to get him special provision as a gifted child in his secondary school.

We couldn't have been more supportive of him, but now he seems more anxious than ever. He cries if he gets something wrong. When he went skiing with the school, he fell over a lot on the first day and then he wouldn't take part for the rest of the week. Now he's saying he wants to opt out of the school production so he can focus on his maths and English. His teacher says that this is not an option, but he really doesn't want to do it – and we don't want to make him unhappy. How can we help him?

A   Your son seems to have developed a fear of failure. He has enjoyed the success of his early years in school, which made him feel special and very clever. Now he's finding it hard to be anything less than the best at what he does – because his whole identity is centred on being top of the class. Your reward and praise for his achievements have inadvertently made this worse, as he doesn't want to let you (or himself) down. He is addicted to success and sees anything less than perfection as failure. When he tries new things and struggles, he would also rather opt out than have to try hard, because he is not used to it.

Give him praise when he tries something new, even if he struggles. That doesn't matter. Encourage him to do things that are outside his comfort zone, like the school production. Talk to him about how he can grow his brain, expand his comfort zone and make progress if he challenges himself, rather than only doing the things he gets high marks for. Don't try to get him labelled as 'gifted', as this may encourage a fixed, rather than a growth, mindset. Help him explore how his intelligence grows when he learns new skills. Help him understand what anxiety is, and show him strategies to handle stress and face his fears.

Give him this book to read!

Chapter 9

Tools for growth

This chapter contains some practical exercises to improve your metacognition and self-regulation. You can grow your thinking skills on purpose, but it takes effort and practice. The more you practice, the more likely you are to find it becomes a habit and a way of life. You can try these activities yourself, or with your children, colleagues or friends. You can find more ideas on my website, www.jackiebeere.com. Please feel free to adapt these ideas and share them through social media, linking to @jackiebeere on Twitter.

In this chapter

1 Mood monitor
2 Reframe thinking cards
3 Comfort zone challenge
4 Timeline plan
5 Visualisation exercise
6 Mindfulness exercises
7 Memory techniques – mastering your memory
8 The happiness manifesto

1. Mood monitor

Use a paper clip to slide along your mood monitor to track your moods and find out your default setting.

Practise metacognition by reflecting on your state of mind. Do this every day to start off with, and note down how your state of mind changes. Start to note how your mood changes at the weekend or at different times of the day.

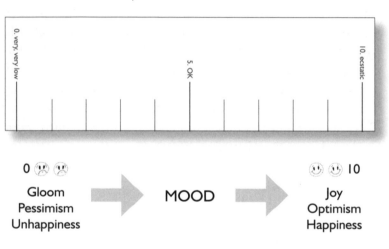

Think about what makes you happy and sad. Be prepared to tweak your thinking to change your mood:

- Try deliberately changing your mood and acting 'as if' you are happy or excited.
- Try writing down what makes you happy or sad. Keep a record of any patterns you notice.
- Try putting other people in a good mood – and see how that affects your mood.

Keep a mood diary for a few days. Make a list of all the things that put you in a great mood. Try doing them more often.

When you have done this for a few weeks, you will be able to take control of your mood much more easily without monitoring your thinking.

2. Reframe thinking cards

Create some reframing cards.

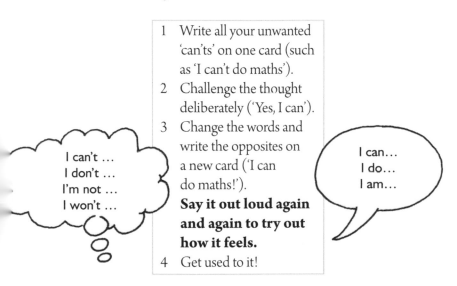

1   Write all your unwanted 'can'ts' on one card (such as 'I can't do maths').
2   Challenge the thought deliberately ('Yes, I can').
3   Change the words and write the opposites on a new card ('I can do maths!'). **Say it out loud again and again to try out how it feels.**
4   Get used to it!

I can't …
I don't …
I'm not …
I won't …

I can…
I do…
I am…

When you are ready, tear up your first card and keep your new card in your pocket. Practise thinking like this regularly.

Write the 'cans' on a memo in your phone or on a business card you carry around with you.

3. Comfort zone challenge

First thoughts – which of these would you do?

Activity	Would do	Might do	Would never do
Parachuting			
Travel abroad alone			
Pick up a spider			
Complain about a product in a shop or café			
Backpack to Australia			
Go to a party alone			
Drive in snow			
Audition for *The X Factor*			
Bungee jump from a cliff			
Deliver a speech to 100 people			
Go on a blind date			
Eat oysters			
Take part in a charity project in the poorest part of Nepal			
Have a filling at the dentist			

This will help you to think about how big your own personal comfort zone is. You may see a pattern in the things that you wouldn't do. Are they all around communication, confidence, food, pain or danger?

Now draw two concentric circles with the inner one representing your 'comfort' zone and the outer one your 'challenge' zone (as shown previously in Figure 5.1). In the comfort zone write everything that you are happy to do in your world. Include hobbies, habits, skills, work activities, etc.

Now think of activities that are currently outside your comfort zone – activities which to varying degrees you would find challenging. They can be simple (such as making a new friend, trying a different food, or going a different way to work). You might include some from your 'might do' or 'would never do' list above. Put those you least want to do furthest away from the inner circle, or even outside the challenge zone in the 'panic' zone. For some people picking up a spider or public speaking might go here – activities which are so challenging they provoke the primitive brain to trigger the fight or flight response.

Your challenge is to widen your comfort zone – permanently. You can do this by challenging yourself to do the things that are outside your comfort zone. The important thing is to keep pushing back the boundaries.

For the bigger things, look back at the reframing exercise. Consider the inner dialogue associated with the challenge and start thinking about it in a different way.

	What are you thinking?	**How could you change that thinking?**
I can't go to the dentist	It's going to hurt I hate him poking around in my mouth I feel trapped I hate the smell and noise of the drill	It won't hurt much, as I'll have an anaesthetic I want my teeth to be healthy I can calm myself by deliberately relaxing I can imagine myself in a different place
I won't do that bungee jump	I may die It's dangerous I can't stand heights The rope could snap Why should I?	There are massive safety precautions It's fun I'll enjoy the adrenalin rush I just need a moment of courage I know I can do this!

Try to tackle something outside your comfort zone every day.

4. Timeline plan

People go to fortune-tellers to try to find out what the future holds for them. You can take a look at your life to date, then plan for all the good things you want to happen. This can help you understand that good times can follow hard times. When you are completing your timeline, be ambitious and brave in your plans. Think big!

Create your own timeline

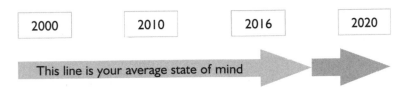

2000   2010   2016   2020

This line is your average state of mind

Draw a pencil line tracing your state of mind through the years since you have been an adult. Do it instinctively, thinking about happy times and challenging moments in those years. Label the highs and lows with events you can remember.

Now add the next five years and place some landmark events that you would like to achieve in those years. Here is an example:

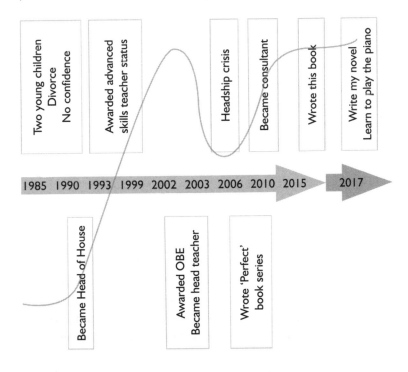

5. Visualisation exercise

Imagine the very best outcome

Thinking on purpose is a challenge. Reframing your limiting beliefs so that you can see things in a different way is hard work. If you want to take a shortcut to managing your thinking, try visualisation.

Your memory and your imagination are closely linked in your brain, and when you imagine something that has happened, or will happen, you experience the same emotions as you did during the real event. When you tell a sad story you feel sad, and when you explain about an amazing success you have achieved, you feel that elation all over again. So the following exercise taps into the way your brain can create a self-fulfilling prophecy by using a mental rehearsal to predict great success.

As experience is mostly constructed in our heads using visual (what you see), auditory (what you hear), and kinaesthetic (what you feel) stimuli, it is useful to construct your visualisation techniques around these. You will notice in this example how we shift the focus across these senses to deepen and strengthen the experience. This helps your brain remember the imagined experience as if it really did happen. So the next time you are in the same situation, your brain remembers how well everything worked out last time and replicates the emotions you created in your imaginary journey.

For example:

The test

You have booked a driving test. It is your third attempt. You have passed the theory and drive very well in all your lessons. Your instructor says you are a good driver. You really need this driving licence for a new job you are starting. You keep thinking the test will be a disaster because in your last test you panicked at a pedestrian crossing and stalled. You need to convince your brain that driving tests are an adventure, and you will enjoy it and pass with flying colours; not just get through it, but demonstrate your excellent skills and confidence on the road.

Try this:

Think of a time when you have been full of confidence and self-control. See yourself, in your mind's eye, looking serene and smiling. Listen to yourself explaining logically and calmly what needs to be done. Feel that strength and resilience inside you as you remember that time when you were at your very best.

Now take this version of yourself and build that positive image a little more. See yourself on your way to the driving test, looking calm, smiling and confident. See yourself relaxed as you travel to the test centre, breathing easily and feeling the flutters inside as excitement and adrenalin that will help you perform well in the test. See yourself walking confidently into the test centre and greeting the examiner. Feel the buzz as you get into the car and sit behind the wheel, knowing you are an excellent driver. Run through the first questions the examiner asks you, and hear yourself answer in a confident, clear voice.

Imagine yourself starting the car and putting it into gear then pulling out while checking your mirrors – feel an amazing sense of calm confidence sweep over you. Go through each possible manoeuvre you undertake: everything is smooth and relaxed. See yourself stop with confidence at roundabouts and traffic lights, then pull away steadily and smoothly. See it all in detail; hear the noise of the other traffic and the examiner talking to you. Feel the excitement and pride when you are challenged with difficult questions but come up with good answers. Switch your attention to the examiner and see him smiling and looking pleased with your driving. As the test comes to an end and you pull up back at the test centre, feel a happy glow inside you as you know what an excellent drive you have just completed. Then the examiner turns to you and says, 'I am pleased to say you have passed your driving test. Well done.' You take the piece of paper that shows you have passed and say thank you. A warm, thrilled buzz of success is waiting to explode inside you.

All this should take at least fifteen minutes, and the pictures you imagine must be big and colourful with a soundtrack of appropriate, confidence-building music. Have a list of your favourite empowering or calming songs to play, to help anchor your positive feelings.

You should imagine what you see, hear and feel so that all your senses are stimulated in this visualisation. After you have mentally rehearsed in this way, when you go for your driving test, your brain will search for information about how it should respond to this challenge, and it will find this memory. If you have done a good job of visualising this experience, the memory will empower you with the same confidence you imagined, and the outcome will become a self-fulfilling prophecy.

Try this visualisation rehearsal for any experience you are nervous about. Get in the habit of imagining things going amazingly well. It will be hard at first, and you will have to remind yourself what to do, but you can tweak your thinking when you catch yourself predicting disaster.

6. Mindfulness exercises

Our minds are full of thoughts. Sometimes it is hard to shut down our thinking and just be in the moment, rather than planning our next activity, reflecting on the past or the future, or worrying about what might happen or what should have happened. Mindfulness helps us develop the ability to be in the moment and give our brains a rest from all that thinking. By practising conscious thinking, we can free ourselves and focus on our positive emotions. Try these exercises.

Clear your mind
Take a piece of white paper and stare at it for a minute. Think of nothing. Clear your mind and banish any intruding thoughts. Just focus on the white and the empty space.

It is hard. It will take practice. However, if you can do this for up to five minutes a day you may find you will be less stressed and more productive because you have given your mind a rest.

Just breathe
Start by breathing mindfully for one minute: really concentrate on feeling the breath enter and then leave your body.

Try breathing in for a count of 7 and breathing out for a count of 11.

Do this for two minutes. With each breath, feel your whole body relax a little more.

Focusing on breathing helps you clear your mind and relaxes you.

Nature study

Choose a flower or leaf in the garden, and just look at it. Look at every detail, concentrate on it and study it for at least two minutes. Stare at it, wonder about it and connect with every detail. Appreciate its unique beauty.

Music immersion

Listen to a piece of music (that has no lyrics) which you haven't heard before. Focus on every detail of the piece. Listen for different instruments and harmonies. Try to immerse yourself in the sounds for a minute or two.

Each of these exercises attempts to get you in the habit of being able to clear your mind and focus on just one thing at a time.

Try to do a mindfulness exercise every day. You can do them in the car (if you are a passenger!) or on a train. If you can make space like this in your head, it is like a colonic irrigation for the mind, and could leave you healthier, happier and more able to cope with all life's demands.

7. Memory techniques – mastering your memory

Being able to remember things is often seen as a badge of honour. It becomes scary when you forget names or important dates or what you went upstairs for! If you are trying to remember something for a test, it is frustrating to consider that you may forget 70% of what you learn today within twenty-four hours if you don't make a special effort to remember it. However, with practice, you can improve your memory.

Your memory works best when you get better at making links between things that connect your learning. This can be visual pictures or connecting ideas using rhyme or rhythm, which stimulates the emotional brain.

Try this. Learn these pairs of nouns:

Sky/Rabbit
Hat/Sausage
Computer/Flower

How did you learn them? Making bright, colourful mental pictures of the objects together will help you remember them. Creating a sentence to link them helps too: for example, 'the sky was full of huge white rabbits'. The more extreme and strange the images you create, the easier it will be for you to remember them.

Rhyming is also a powerful way to help you remember things. Here is a shopping list to memorise:

Ice cream
Carrots
Potatoes
Baked beans
Soap
Chocolate
Biscuits
Bread
Orange juice
Pork chops

Take a minute to memorise the list, then see how many you can recall.

Now create a wacky rhyme for each word and a mad image to go with it:

- Ice cream – scream (you could picture the ice cream forming the image of a huge scream, as in the famous picture)
- Carrots – maggots (picture carrots with huge maggots chomping away on them)
- Potatoes – crows (picture crows sitting on a mound of potatoes)
- Baked beans – jeans (picture a tin of beans pouring over your best jeans)

You get the idea. How many can you remember now?

Tip: learning people's names is easier if you use alliteration. For example, Gentle Joe or Serious Sarah, Perfect Paul, Mad Matthew, Crafty Catherine. Be careful you don't find yourself labelling personal qualities and thereby your perceptions of people!

Use mnemonics to help your memory

This means using letters to make up phrases that help you remember. For example, it's hard to remember how to spell 'necessary', but Never Eat Cakes: Eat Salad, Sandwiches And Remain Young is easier to remember.

Tip: mental pictures, associations, mnemonics and rhyming techniques are all aides-memoires. Advertisers know this – can you remember any radio advertising slogans? Why did you learn them? Did you need to, or did you just assimilate them by accident?

Review is an essential part of learning and memory. If you top up your learning on a regular basis, you will find it stays with you.

8. The happiness manifesto

Your definition of success and happiness may be passing exams, getting a well-paid job, being beautiful, or having lots of material possessions. However, you may have all of this and still be unhappy.

You need to be clear about what makes you happy. (It might not mean the same thing as being successful.) Create your own personal success manifesto. Here is a real-life example to consider.[1]

Happiness is	Is not
Wanting to get up and start the day	Getting through the day
Feeling my values and beliefs are in tune with my daily activities	Feeling my values are being challenged by what I have to do
Being in 'flow': doing something really well with concentration and love	Being part of a faceless commuter herd
Causing minimal harm to the world – animals and ecosystem	Rushing, checking emails, responding to messages, lining things up, ticking off jobs then filling up the next to-do list ....
Feeling good, energised, calm and fit	Feeling judged by my peers, superiors, family or society
Harmony between my emotional and logical responses	Yearning for tranquillity in reactive situations

---

1   Thanks to Rob for this idea.

Happiness is	Is not
Exploring new ideas, open to new ways of thinking and learning new skills	Feeling boxed in and unable to express my beliefs
Being *me*	Being used or feeling I have to pretend to be someone else

Try making your own happiness manifesto. Check your lifestyle against it and see if you are living the life that can make you most happy. If not, what can you do about it?

In the first column, start by thinking about how you want to feel. Then compare this with how you actually feel on a daily basis. Once you are clear about what you want and what you don't want, you can work out how to take the first steps towards a happier life.

You can use this type of table if it helps:

What I want	What it feels like now	What steps can I take to make a change?
An example Wanting to get up and start the day	Getting through the day	Consider what aspect of my day feels less appealing and make some changes

Top tips for thinking on purpose

1 Know yourself – be aware of your default mood setting so you can adjust it and tune in to how your unique brain influences your thinking.
2 Now listen to your thinking – the language, the sentiment, so you can ...
3 Challenge and reframe your thinking, if it isn't helpful.
4 Make the people around you happier – deliberately.
5 Challenge your comfort zone every day.
6 STOP. Be in the moment for a few minutes each day, take time to see the good stuff around you.
7 Reboot your body and your mind by smiling, singing, stretching or walking tall.

References and further reading

Books and articles

Achor, S. (2010) *The Happiness Advantage: The seven principles of positive psychology that fuel success and performance at work*. London: Virgin Books.

Amen, D.G. (1998) *Change Your Brain, Change Your Life*. New York: Three Rivers Press.

BBC News (2011) Brain changes seen in cabbies who take 'The Knowledge' (8 December). Available at: http://www.bbc.co.uk/news/health-16086233.

Beere, J. (2007) *The Learner's Toolkit*. Carmarthen: Crown House Publishing.

Brown, B. (2015) *Rising Strong*. London: Penguin Random House.

Burton, G. and Dimbleby, R. (1988) *Between Ourselves: An introduction to interpersonal communication*. London: Arnold.

Canfield, J. (2005) *The Success Principles*. London: HarperCollins.

Carey, N. (2011) *The Epigenetics Revolution*. London: Icon Books.

Children's Society (2015) *The Good Childhood Report 2015*. Available at: www.childrenssociety.org.uk/sites/default/files/TheGoodChildhoodReport2015.pdf.

Collins, J. (2001) *Good to Great*. London: Random House Business.

Covey, S. (1989) *The 7 Habits of Highly Effective People*. London: Simon & Schuster.

Curran, A. (2008) *The Little Book of Big Stuff About the Brain*. Carmarthen: Crown House Publishing.

Duhigg, C. (2012) *The Power of Habit*. London: Random House.

Dweck, C. (2000) *Self-theories: Their role in motivation, personality, and development*. New York: Psychology Press.

Dweck, C. (2007) *Mindset: The new psychology of success*. New York: Random House.

FitzGerald, E. (1989) *Rubáiyát of Omar Khayyám*. London: Penguin.

Fleming, N.D. (2001) *Teaching and Learning Styles: VARK strategies*, 5th edn. Published by the author, Christchurch, New Zealand.

Frank, L. (2007) *Mindfield: How brain science is changing our world*. Oxford: One World Publications.

Gardner, H. (1993) *Frames of Mind: The theory of multiple intelligences*, 2nd edn. London: Fontana Press.

Gilovich, T., Husted Medvec, V. and Savitsky, K. (2000) 'The Spotlight Effect in Social Judgment: An Egocentric Bias in Estimates of the Salience of One's Own Actions and Appearance', *Journal of Personality and Social Psychology*, 78 (2): 211–222.

Gladwell, M. (2008) *Outliers: The story of success*. London: Penguin.

Goleman, D. (1996) *Emotional Intelligence: Why it can matter more than IQ*. London: Bloomsbury.

Goleman, D. (2004) *Working with Emotional Intelligence*. London: Bloomsbury.

Goleman, D. (2014) *Focus: The hidden driver of excellence*. London: Bloomsbury.

Goleman, D., Boyatzis, R. and Mckee, A. (2002) *The New Leaders*. London: Time Warner.

Greenfield, S. (2000) *The Private Life of the Brain*. London: Penguin.

Grinder, J. and Bandler, R. (1981) *Frogs into Princes: Neuro linguistic programming*. Moab, UT: Real People Press.

Harris, S. (2010) *The Moral Landscape*. London: Bantam Press.

HH Dalai Lama and Cutler, H.C. (1999) *The Art of Happiness: A handbook for living*. London: Hodder.

Higgins, S., Katsipataki, M., Kokotsaki, D., Coleman, R., Major, L.E. and Coe, R. (2014) The Sutton Trust-Education Endowment Foundation Teaching and Learning Toolkit. London: Education Endowment Foundation.

Hymer, B. and Gershon, M. (2014) *Growth Mindset Pocketbook*. Alresford: Teachers' Pocketbooks.

Isen, A.M. (1999) Positive affect. In T. Dalgleish and M. Power (eds), *Handbook of Cognition and Emotion*. Chichester: John Wiley & Sons, pp. 521–540.

Jaekel, J., Eryigit-Madzwamuse, S. and Wolke, D. (2016) 'Preterm Toddlers' Inhibitory Control Abilities Predict Attention Regulation and Academic Achievement at Age 8 Years', *Journal of Pediatrics* (February) 169: 87–92.

James, O. (2007) *Affluenza*. London: Vermilion.

James, O. (2016) *Not in Your Genes*. London: Vermilion.

Jung, C.G. (1989 [1962]) *Memories, Dreams, Reflections*, A. Jaffé (ed), R. Winston and C. Winston (trs). New York: Vintage.

Jung, C.G. (2002[1958]) *The Undiscovered Self*. Abingdon: Routledge Classics.

Jung, C.G. (2015 [1973]) *C.G. Jung Letters: Volume 1 1906–1950*, G. Adler and A. Jaffé (eds), R.F.C. Hull (trs), Abingdon: Routledge.

Kahneman, D. (2011) *Thinking, Fast and Slow*. London: Penguin.

Karpman, S. (1968) 'Fairy tales and script drama analysis', *Transactional Analysis Bulletin*, 7(26): 39–43.

Korzybski, A. (1933) *Science and Sanity*. Lakeville, CN: Institute of General Semantics.

MacLean, P.D. (1973) *A Triune Concept of the Brain and Behavior*. Toronto: University of Toronto Press.

Merlevede, P., Bridoux, D. and Vandamme, R. (1997) *7 Steps to Emotional Intelligence*. Carmarthen: Crown House Publishing.

O'Connor, J. and Seymour, J. (1990) *Introducing NLP*. San Francisco, CA: Thorsons.

Peters, S. (2012) *The Chimp Paradox*. London: Vermilion.

Revell, J. and Norman, S. (1997) *In Your Hands: NLP for teaching and learning*. London: Saffire Press.

Reynolds, L. and Birdwell, J. (2015) *Mind Over Matter* (Demos). Available at: www.demos.co.uk/project/mind-over-matter/.

Robbins, A. (1991) *Awaken the Giant Within*. New York: Fireside.

Rose Charvet, S. (1995) *Words that Change Minds*. Dubuque, IA: Kendall/ Hunt Publishing Co.

Siebert, A. (2005) *The Resiliency Advantage*. San Francisco, CA: Berrett-Koehler.

Syed, M. (2011) *Bounce*. London: Fourth Estate.

Thaler, R.H. and Sunstein, C.R. (2009) *Nudge: Improving decisions about health, wealth and happiness*. London: Penguin.

Tolstoy, L. (2002 [1910]) *Path of Life*, M. Cole (trs). Hauppauge, NY: Nova Science Publishers.

Watts, P. (2015) *Echopraxia*. London: Head of Zeus Ltd.

Webb, L. (2013) *Resilience: How to cope when everything around you keeps changing*. Chichester: Capstone.

Websites

Chabris and Simon, The Invisible Gorilla – www.theinvisiblegorilla.com/gorilla_experiment.html

Discover Magazine – http://discovermagazine.com/2011/mar/10-numbers-the-nervous-system

Forbes – www.forbes.com/sites/work-in-progress/2012/12/20/deepak-chopra-on-your-super-brain work-stress-and-creativity/#2715e4857a0b2eba26f0297d

Jackie Beere – www.jackiebeere.com

Live bold and bloom – http://liveboldandbloom.com/05/values/list-of-values

Mindset works – http://community.mindsetworks.com/the-growth-mindset-digest-issue-37-april-2016

Prison Reform Trust – www.prisonreformtrust.org.uk/projectsresearch/mentalhealth

Rainy brain sunny brain – www.rainybrainsunnybrain.com/bbc-horizon/

REBT Network – www.rebtnetwork.org/library/ideas.html

Resiliency centre resiliency quiz – http://resiliencyquiz.com/index.shtml

The human memory – http://www.human-memory.net/brain_neurons.html

Typoglycemic creator – www.leapbeyond.com/ric/scrambler/

Acknowledgements

I'd like to thank some special people who helped and inspired me to write this book. Firstly, my friend Rhona who took an interest in the book from the very beginning when we spent hours walking and talking about our mutual fascination with the human condition. Her generous advice and feedback helped me move my ideas forward. My great feedback team included my daughter Carrie and her friend Sangeeta who both encouraged me throughout, supplying ideas which also make this book relevant and useful for young working women. My neighbour Jill deserves thanks for her constant belief in this book, as do my best friend Gill and sister Leslie for their enthusiastic support, and Terri for being my growth mindset role model!

I want to thank my brother Robert for his useful insights and for successfully putting some of the strategies in the book into practice, and also for his brilliant encouragement throughout the process of writing. It is better because of his input and I loved sharing ideas with him.

Thanks must also go to everyone at Crown House Publishing, who is so supportive and patient. If it hadn't been for Caroline's persistence, this book would probably never have happened. Having worked for 30 years teaching and trying to convince friends and colleagues that the way you think makes all the difference, it was wonderful to read Carol Dweck's research on growth mindsets and finally have all the evidence. Thank you to everyone I taught and trained, from whom I have learnt so much.

Finally, a huge thank you has to go to my fantastic husband and rock, John, who made sense of my ramblings and who worked tirelessly to make my writing better.

The hardest job in the world is to be a great parent, so thanks to my lovely daughters who continually inspire me to grow. This book is for the children of the future, such as my wonderful grandchildren, Lyla, Taran and Josh, who have reminded me about how we can all lead happier lives, be less afraid of being judged and be a little bit braver.

Thanks to everyone else I know who helps keep me optimistic. As Mum and Dad always told me, most people are good and the world is a much better place than it used to be.

Jackie Beere MBA OBE

Jackie worked as a newspaper journalist before starting a career in teaching and school leadership. She rose from supply teacher to become head teacher of a large, successful secondary school, and was awarded the OBE in 2002 for developing innovative learning programmes for students and teachers. Since 2006 she has been training teachers and school and business leaders in the latest strategies for learning, developing emotionally intelligent leadership and growth mindsets.

Jackie is now the author of several bestselling books on teaching, learning and coaching, as well as being a qualified Master Practitioner in NLP.